What the me
are saying ab

MW01075442

"If you or someone you know is struggling with OCD, this book is a must-have! Offering an open, candid, and insightful look at how OCD can wreak havoc and devastation, Jim's journey is captured in a heartfelt, sincere, genuine, and compassionate manner. Sending a clear message that OCD is treatable through inspiration and countless tips, his ability to turn tragedy into advocacy will undoubtedly offer hope for others."

~ Dr. Robin Zasio, PsyD, LCSW,
The Anxiety Treatment Center, Scientific Advisory
Board/Clinical Advisory Board/Speakers Bureau/
BTTI Faculty: The International OCD Foundation

"A must-read for anyone who has OCD or lives with someone who does. As a clinical psychologist who helps people suffering from OCD and related issues, I recognize how important it is for my clients to realize that they are not alone or unique, normalizing what can seem 'crazy.' Reading this personal account of a pioneer in the field of OCD can accomplish that as well as provide inspiration and tools to do the work of recovery."

~ Donald Dufford, PhD, Licensed Clinical Psychologist,
Director, Anxiety Treatment Services

"James Callner has courageously shared his journey to reach out to the millions of people suffering with OCD. His book is inspirational and offers wisdom and techniques for recovery. Highly recommended for anyone who may feel alone in their struggle with OCD. Thank you, James, for sharing your journey with the world."

~ Sharon Davies, MBACP,
Director of The OCD Treatment Centre, Taunton, England

"Get inside the head and heart of an unabashedly honest and courageous OCD sufferer whose sharing of his historical walk and healing transformation gives hope to those suffering in silence."

~ Ron Wiebe, retired psychotherapist
and organizational consultant

"James Callner's book brings together a lifetime of discovery—what works and what doesn't—in OCD recovery. His approach is kind, no-nonsense, and straightforward. He delivers powerful insights into the secrets of living a wholesome life of recovery from OCD. In my 30-year career as a psychologist with OCD, I have worked with hundreds of patients with OCD and trained hundreds of professionals in optimal OCD treatment methods. *It's a Matter of Trust* has earned a prominent place on my desk where I plan to use it as a regular reference text. I hope you will too!"

~ Christian R. Komor, PsyD, The OCD Recovery Center

"This is a fantastic book for OCD sufferers. James Callner speaks in a friendly, familiar, and knowledgeable way that is sure to provide others with a deep sense of comfort. The fact that this is a personal story of his struggles with the condition only adds to its charm, whilst offering wise, skilled, and applicable tools that could help many break free from the grips of OCD."

~ Craig Shirley, BSc (Hons) Psychology, Senior Therapist
and Co-founder of The OCD Treatment Centre

"More than a self-help memoir, this book serves as an encyclopedia for treating OCD. James Callner's easy-to-read book will not only help those challenged with OCD but depression and anxiety disorders as well. He speaks from experience and from the heart. Highly recommended. "

~ Phil Kavanaugh, MD, Psychiatrist,
Johns Hopkins School of Medicine

"James Callner has written such a wonderful, encouraging, and honest book filled with hope, strength, and solutions!"

~ Hasanna Fletcher, Licensed Marriage and Family Therapist

"James Callner has shared several anecdotes and personal tools and techniques that have helped him to disengage from the terror of OCD in his mind and brain, which are inspirational for sufferers alike. I would personally like to salute Jim for sharing his brave, touching, and inspirational story along with his unconditional, tireless effort to continue to offer compassion, hope, and healing for those in need."

~ Karen Buckingham, OCD specialist
(Reg MBACP), OCD Therapy Clinic UK

"With amazing courage, James Callner reveals to us the details of his personal journey with OCD. He does so to try to reach the hearts, minds, and spirits of those who suffer, on a daily basis, with OCD. Those who have not yet received a formal diagnosis of OCD as well as those who have will immediately recognize their own symptoms of OCD in Jim's vivid accounts of his struggles with the disorder. And I have no doubt they will heave a sigh of relief to know that they are not the only ones on the face of this planet who experience thoughts and behavior that can be bizarre and frightening. More importantly, James provides incredible hope for living with and healing from OCD. He provides the reader with a virtual arsenal of methods, strategies, and ideas to fight OCD from such evidence-based treatments as exposure and response prevention and medication to more personal coping strategies and techniques. In short, I believe this book has the capacity to positively impact the lives of scores of individuals with OCD. Bravo, Mr. Callner, for opening your soul to others so they may heal. "

~ Dr. Gail B. Adams, author of
Students with OCD: A Handbook for School Personnel

How people recovering from OCD
are celebrating *It's a Matter of Trust* ...

"James Callner captures the experience of having OCD from a place where only a fellow sufferer would truly identify. His honest and candid reflections of living a life with OCD inspire hope, recovery, and trust to all of us who know OCD from the insider's point of view. *It's a Matter of Trust* is a must-read for anyone whose life is touched by OCD. "

~ Richard, 56 years old

"An insightful and honest read of a personal journey into the debilitating disorder of OCD that shows amazing courage and strength."

~ Jo, 43 years old

"James Callner knows about OCD firsthand. As someone who has suffered with this painful and often misunderstood disorder, he shares the very important messages of daily practice with ERP/CBT, trust, hope, love, and compassion as mechanisms to overcome and manage OCD. His guidance have been a true blessing in my life."

~ Jeff, 37 years old

"The only thing I can say is 'Wow!' It's incredible that James Callner decided to share his story with us all. It's one of the most touching things when people share their pain and experiences. The way he describes how it feels to live with compulsions, intrusive thoughts, and anxiety is simply correct, and I hope it will make a lot of people understand OCD a little more. Reading this gives me a lot of strength for my upcoming therapy. You are right. It's all about trust!"

~ Claudia, 19 years old

"This book is an excellent read. The author discusses his experience with OCD and how it has affected him over the past three decades. He describes a holistic approach (using a variety of methods) that would be useful to anyone facing this disorder. I am an OCD sufferer, and it has helped me to be open to using multiple approaches to manage it. It has also helped me to learn trust and willingness and to allow myself to feel whatever I'm feeling. I've also learned a new point of view of looking at things more positively in life. I would recommend this book for everyone with OCD to have in their arsenal."

~ Megan, 32 years old

"I heard someone once say of their life experience while managing a debilitating illness, 'You won't get it until you get it!' In other words, people wouldn't be able to understand what it was like to live with their illness unless they could experience the pain of that illness firsthand. Mr. Callner's memoir helped me 'get'—to a much deeper extent than I ever have—what it's like for my mother to live with her OCD. Callner's moving story, told with a clear narrative, provided deep insight for me, which has given me not only greater empathy but a toolbox of imparted wisdom with which to help support my mother. I'll be gifting a copy of this book to my mother and a couple of our friends too!"

~ Brittany, 25 years old

"In this book the author describes powerful methods of how he overcame the grips of obsessive-compulsive disorder. Applying some of James Callner's own techniques myself has shown that there is truth to the saying, 'Sometimes when things do not work, don't try harder, try different.' Whether you are just learning about OCD or on your own path towards management, this book is for you!"

~ Sarah, 38 years old

It's a Matter of Trust

Hope & Solutions for OCD and How I Got Better

James Callner

with Jan Baumgartner

ISBN-13: 978-0-9980729-0-6

Cover and interior design and editing by Joanne Shwed, Backspace Ink (www.BackspaceInk.com)

Disclaimer: This book is based on my life with obsessive compulsive disorder (OCD) and my personal experiences and ongoing recovery from OCD and anxiety. Overdramatizations of any events are solely based on my experience and memory of the past. I am not a therapist or psychiatrist, and all suggestions should be reviewed with your health care specialist.

This book is dedicated to the most important individuals in my recovery: the two men who— with compassion, humor, kindness, and love— helped me to help myself back to life.

Phil Kavanaugh, MD, retired psychiatrist
and
Ron Wiebe, retired licensed clinical social worker

Contents

Acknowledgements 17

Before You Start This Book 19

Introduction: How the Journey Began 21

Chapter 1: OCD Saved My Life 25

Chapter 2: The Power of Willingness and Trust 37

Chapter 3: Surrender.. 47

    Surrendering to Anxiety 51

    Letting Go of Control to Get Control 53

    Feel the Feelings 55

    Surrendering to What Is 56

Chapter 4: Pain Forced Me to Change 59

Chapter 5: Letting Go of Control:
The Power of Popcorn... 67

    The Steps 72

    The "G" Word 74

Chapter 6: Living on My Own...................................... 79

    The Attempt to Quiet the Mind 82

    The Obsessive Committee 85

    Moving In 87

The Park and the Truth..89

My Chicken Treatment..92

"You Can Start Your Day Anytime"....................................94

Chapter 7: Ask and Honor 97

Telling the Truth..100

Relationships and Answering the Unanswerable Question 101

Honor the Feelings of Others 107

Chapter 8: The Dark Days: Finding the Light in the Darkness 109

Light Made the Shift...112

Checking on Highway 9 114

The Bathroom Flood 119

The Desk 122

What Does OCD Feel Like? 126

Chapter 9: "You're Late!" The Power of Honesty............129

The Courage to Be Honest..134

Chapter 10: 12 Steps to *The Touching Tree* Movie........137

The Power of Listening..141

Higher Self 143

12-Step Connection 144

Progress Not Perfection...147

Projection Makes Perception...150

Service to Others..154

Chapter 11: "Me, Being Me, and Letting You See Me" ...159

Chapter 12: You Do the Best You Can Given the Conditions You Are Under............165

   The Harming Fear 168

   "You Give Me Strength" 172

   Letter to Cousin Joey 178

   The Bottom Line 182

Chapter 13: OCD Challenged Me to Face My Fears 185

   Thought Replacement 189

   Why It Works for Me 193

   The Higher-Power Concept............199

   The Bully 200

   CBT/ERP and the Shower 202

   Going for It............203

   Helpful Words 206

Chapter 14: Mindfulness: The Ultimate Anchor............209

   Mindfulness and Mindful Awareness 213

   Using Mindful Awareness to Stop Checking 214

   Using Mindful Awareness to Let Go of Control 216

   The Complainer 218

Chapter 15: Love Heals 221

   There Are Only Two Emotions: Love and Fear 226

   Helpful Philosophies 227

   Larry's Love 230

   I Choose Love 233

Chapter 16: What Really Helped Me? 237

  Can You Laugh at OCD? 240

  "Don't Label Me!" 243

  Teachers of Spirituality.......................................244

  Simple Breathing Meditation 250

  Medications and Supplements 254

  Energy Healing..256

  Exercise 258

  Jim's 80-20 Suggestion 259

  Nutrition 261

  Jeanine's "Everything but the Kitchen Sink" Smoothie Recipe......263

  Self-talk and Affirmations...................................264

  Reasonable Reason to Change 268

  Nothing Changes if Nothing Changes 270

  Hope 272

  The Opposite of Fear Is Trust 273

Chapter 17: How I Am Now, Living with OCD 275

Chapter 18: How Do We Trust?...............................279

My Anxiety First-Aid List....................................287

Help and Hope Resources 289

  Foundations and Associations 289

  Treatment Centers and Online Help 289

  12-Step Programs..290

James Callner Films and Coaching Videos 291

Recommended Books 293

About the Author: James Callner 295

About the Editor: Jan Baumgartner 297

Acknowledgments

I have been so blessed in my life to have the support and love of so many people, and the word "acknowledgment" is too small of a word for how I feel. Appreciation, gratitude, and thankfulness are more accurate.

Obsessive compulsive disorder (OCD) is such a tough, challenging, devastating disorder, not only for the sufferer but for everyone in the family. My parents saw their son suffering horribly. They did not turn away, shame, or judge me; instead, they embraced me, loved me, and found the best help for me. I am eternally grateful to my parents and the rest of my family.

In addition to my family, I will be forever grateful to my friends, who stuck by me without judgment or shame. While they may not have understood OCD completely, they chose to not define me by my illness but accept me as "Jim who has his challenges," like everyone else. For me, that is the very meaning of friendship.

Thank you to those who stuck by me through it all: Jeff Bengford; Paul Cosentino; Kimberly Schwartz; Phil Mancini; Mary Rogers; Michael Morris, LMFT; Scott Brown; Joni Rodgers; Jeff DeClue; Bryan Moriarty; Stephen Turturici; Ginger Drake; Brad Weisberg; Bruce Des Les Dernier; Amy Zsadanyi-Yale; Gerald Carter; Jack Senteney; Chris Komor, PhD; Jim Berkheimer; Gail Adams, EdD; Steve Longstreth;

Bob Moore; David Espar; Preston Connick; Wah Ho Chan; Spencer Commons; Tom Bullock; Jeff Risk; Paula Sneddon; Steve DeFrisco; D. Jeffery Duckham, MD; Hasanna Flether, LMFT; Sharon Davies, MBACP; Flor Silva; Yeni Escobar; and so many others. (You know who you are.)

And to a mental health tech named Dennis and the staff of Therapeutic Community One (TC-1) in 1982.

My gratitude extends to my many students of over 35 years and staff at West Valley College in Saratoga, California, who did not shame, blame, or judge me for my disability but embraced me as a teacher. They opened their hearts to accept me as I am.

My appreciation and thanks to Jan Baumgartner, without whom this book would not have been written. Jan edited, wordsmithed, and collaborated with me to help make this book what it is—a book about trust, help, and hope. And many thanks to my proofreaders: P. Lucido-Martin, MS; Marty Bengford; and Jeanine Sande.

My appreciation to Joanne Shwed at Backspace Ink for cover and interior design and editing.

Lastly, my love and gratitude to the woman who has helped me with this book in every way—and, more importantly, she has taught me that relationships are about helping each other heal: my dear wife Jeanine Sande.

Before You Start This Book

In this book, every chapter gives you some hope. The book evolves from my story of OCD into philosophies, suggestions, techniques, and methods of how I got better. As the book progresses, you will see more and more helpful tools for your own recovery. However, if you are experiencing anxiety or panic right now, go directly to My Anxiety First-Aid List at the back of the book, page 287. I hope it will help.

INTRODUCTION

How the Journey Began

Just a little history to get you started ...
I was blessed to find my passion (acting in plays, making films) at an early age and to have spent my professional life as a Theatre Arts & Film teacher at West Valley College in Saratoga, California. I started teaching in 1977 at the young age of 24. And I retired 37 years later.

During my early years as a college teacher, I was in a relationship with Jan Baumgartner, my amazing collaborator. While with Jan, my love for and dedication to her was absolutely authentic. However, I had a secret that began before I met her. My horrible, secret, sex addiction was very real. After a year or so of sharing a home with Jan and leading a double life, my secret and the sex addiction that was driving it were coming to a head. I was at a breaking point—literally, a break*down* point. I was overwhelmed with fear, panic, shame, guilt, and confusion.

By 1982, all of that fear, guilt, and confusion led to the start of OCD behavior. Listen to me: The sex addiction did not *cause* the OCD. But it did *trigger* the neurobiological disorder that may have been dormant in my genetic makeup.

I began the hand-washing ritual. And I remember Jan walking in once and seeing my hands raw from scrubbing, blood running down the drain. I had to confess to Jan what had been going on and about my addiction. She had no idea of this double and destructive life that I had been living. Thankfully, no physical harm had come to her or to me during that promiscuous and dangerous time. But the mental stress and anguish that came with living with a person she thought she knew and trusted, and then realizing that person's huge, secret life, caused her to feel anger, betrayal, and abandonment. Who was this man she had been living with? Who was I? Neither of us knew.

The relationship ended. And I ended up in the hospital. Jan picked up the pieces of her life, eventually moving to San Francisco and meeting her future husband. Jan moved on. I started on my journey called "recovery."

Here is where the odd (but not so odd) part comes in. Nearly 30 years had gone by, and I was now married. Out of curiosity, I searched the Internet to see what had happened to Jan and what she was doing. I found out that she was living on the coast of Maine. I also found numerous articles and essays that she had written. I hesitated, and then took the risk to e-mail her. To my amazement, she e-mailed back, and we reconnected by phone. She was in her late 40s and I in my 50s. Our lives and paths had not crossed in decades.

During the last few years before I contacted her, I had been putting together a self-help book on OCD, which would later become this book. I told her about it, and she asked if I'd like to contribute any articles on OCD to be published online. I did, and Jan edited these articles prior to their publication.

As this was my first book and dear to my heart, I had been looking for an editor who could wordsmith my sentences and my ideas and feelings; someone who could collaborate with me. I was looking for someone who knew more than I did about writing a book. My background was in writing screenplays and in making films, not in writing articles or books, which I found to be extremely difficult.

One night, at our dining room table, my wise wife Jeanine said, "Why don't you ask Jan to edit your book?"

"Are you *crazy*? After what I put that woman through? Now I should ask her to edit a book about my life, including a recap of that sex addiction?"

Jeanine looked at me with a smile—as very intuitive women often do—and simply said, "Yes, I think she would be perfect. Give her a call."

I mustered up the nerve and sheepishly asked Jan, "Would you ever consider editing my memoir?"

Here's the part that shows the character and loving nature of my friend Jan Baumgartner. As I recall, there wasn't even a pause on the other end of the phone when she simply said, "It would be an honor."

My eyes teared up. I could not believe it. I had to make sure that she fully understood what she'd be in for and what I'd be writing about.

"Wouldn't it freak you out? Everything we went through? It's not pretty."

Jan said calmly, "Jim, that was nearly 30 years ago. That was a lifetime ago for me. I've been through so much life and living beyond you. It would be my honor to help you with your book. Besides, who better to help you with this than someone who was with you at the beginning of it all?"

So, I decided to trust—and the journey began.

CHAPTER 1

OCD Saved My Life

The only way over fear is through it.

~ Phil Kavanaugh, MD

“At 30, you'll start growing up.”

That's what I was told in so many words by my psychiatrist in 1982 while I was in TC-1, a psychiatric unit at Good Samaritan Hospital in San Jose, California. I was 29 and admitted for what was then called a nervous breakdown with the onset of severe OCD. Without a doubt, it was the turning point of my life—a “secret life” that was previously filled with crippling anxiety and a dangerous sexual addiction.

Coming from an upper middle-class home in Wisconsin and transported to California when I was nine, I was not a typical child of the '60s generation; that is, I was a bit different than most of my friends in school. While they were listening to the Beatles and the Rolling Stones, I was listening to jazz, Brasil '66, and Burt Bacharach. While they were smoking, drinking, or popping a pill, I shied away, never wanting or feeling the need to get “high” or drunk.

Instead, my drug of choice was being on stage. I was in almost all the school plays. Acting was my true “high.” My father, an educational film director, included me in his movies. Working on many of his sets, I learned invaluable lessons in all aspects of filmmaking. I began to make my own films, experimenting and taking advantage of my father's contacts.

Looking back at those high school days, I remember how anxious I was, holding tightly to my script until my entrance on stage. But soon the laughs would come, the applause and the recognition. It was exhilarating. I knew I could do it and do it well.

Until I entered college, I was the school star. Voted "most talented" in the high school yearbook, my ego was in full bloom. Then college came around, and I was one among 28,000 students. The theater department was large. And, to my shock, I was very small. No one seemed to recognize my talent. Suddenly, all of the compliments I enjoyed from high school disappeared. My inflated ego took a rapid free-fall. I was not in one formal play in the four years of college or the two years of graduate school.

I changed my major to radio-television-film because, in my mind, those students seemed to have a lot more fun. Once established in that department, I started to move into what I call the "Woody Allen approach to movie making." (Woody Allen once said that he liked being in his own movies rather than in nightly theater appearances because he didn't have to be there.) So, I put myself in a few of my own independent films, in which I directed and acted, thus avoiding the anxiety of having to be at the theater every night. With my confidence intact, I began winning film-festival awards and eventually earned a master's degree in theater with a special emphasis in film.

During this time, however, I was not disconnected from the world of theater. I was fortunate enough to land a job with the city, writing and directing plays for a local community teen theater. That job kept me in the land of theater while my father kept me in the land of film. I was happy working in both art forms. But I was an anxious guy.

Back in my youth of the 1960s and '70s, there was no word in my vocabulary that would define certain feelings like overwhelming fear. Without a doubt, I knew what anxiety "felt" like. But, because that term was then unfamiliar to me, my older brother Dale and I used to call these fears "the scaries." I knew all too well what this onset of anxiety felt like. And I would do almost anything to rid myself of these feelings of intense fear. Little did I know that, in my case, "the scaries" would progress into "the panics," and then into addiction.

I was in my early 20s when, one night after a rehearsal, my technical director asked if I wanted to go to a massage parlor. I was totally naive. I thought those places only existed in Reno—Mustang Ranch, legal prostitution—but in the Bay Area? In Santa Cruz? He combed through the phone book under the heading of "massage." I was shocked. Page after page listed massage parlors. But he was looking for those that used "massage parlor" as a front. He made a couple of calls, asked coded-type questions, and off we went to Santa Cruz in his 1971 truck.

The massage parlor experience was what you would expect, yet I was stunned at the simplicity of sex for pay and the attention. This dysfunctional and false attention and "love" hooked me like any drug. I went back the next day, alone. Seemingly, I had found a magic cure-all to relieve my anxiety at any given time—and all it took was a short drive and a pocketful of cash. At the time, I knew nothing of addiction. In my naiveté, I associated addiction only with drugs and alcohol.

While the addiction progressed, and the search for new and different sexual experiences escalated, I had the gnawing feeling that this high-risk behavior would lead to some form of danger in my life. However, like so many addicts, the compelling urge overrode my logic. And it was always the same. I felt excited and charged up going; then, heading home after a sex show or massage parlor visit, I would feel horrible, saying to myself, "I have to stop." That intense craving would reappear, triggered by anxiety or a stressor in my life. And, like pushing a replay button, off I'd go to get my fix, taking care of the anxiety with the addiction. With the exception of a few friends who knew of my actions and were similarly addicted, maintaining and covering up this destructive and dark secret consumed my life.

At the beginning of the AIDS (acquired immune deficiency syndrome) epidemic in the early '80s, the chaos of a secret life and the endless lies came to an end and, ultimately, saved my life. I was arrested twice during those years, never serving jail time but coming frighteningly close. In those days, police were raiding porno shops and shows and arresting any and all who happened to be there. The penalty for my arrests was nothing more than fines and community service. But these incidents proved mortifying to me. Others had always seen or characterized me as "together," talented, and successful. That perception was a heavy burden to carry. And—because of my secret addiction—it was only partly true.

I believe, as do my two therapists of 28 years, that the arrests did not cause me to have OCD. But they pulled my biological trigger for OCD. Most likely, I was genetically predisposed. The trauma of being arrested, however, and the stress and buildup of guilt and shame, finally led to a breakdown and the onset of full, clinical OCD. All of the previous defense mechanisms that I had used against my fears were lost. They had finally broken down.

So, why do I believe that OCD saved my life? If I had stayed on the path of sexual addiction, I may very well have contracted any number of sexually transmitted diseases, including AIDS, and passed it on in my secret life.

I was about to begin a new chapter that was more powerful, challenging, and terrifying than anything I had ever experienced.

At age 29, I sat in TC-1, with others going though various mental health challenges, and felt as though I had been thrown in jail. (Please note that TC-1 was not an intensive OCD program like what is offered today; it included people needing help with a variety of mental health issues.) I had lost my relationship with my girlfriend, my job, my apartment, and my friends. My old friend—sex—had taken a hike and was now replaced with an overwhelming fear of sex. And, if that wasn't enough, I had a progressive and debilitating disorder called OCD.

Day and night, obsessions of harming, or fears that I had already harmed my girlfriend or family with my addictive behavior, were running rampant and wreaking havoc with my mind. My obsessions and phobias about germs and contamination resulted in severe hand-washing, sometimes up to nine hours a day.

While I was not suicidal, the overwhelming horrors of OCD led me to pray for God to take me. Subconsciously, and in hindsight, I must have believed that there was some light at the end of this darkness. But still I prayed for the brutal pain to go away.

Like many people, I experienced anxiety and panic as physical pain. It felt like electricity bolting through my body or a sensation of extreme fluctuations of hot and cold. During that time, it was a daily and consistent nightmare.

Weeks went by in TC-1. My dedicated psychiatrist came to the unit each day, including weekends, gently and sometimes firmly moving me toward taking risks and facing my fears, using what we now call exposure response prevention therapy (ERPT), or simply ERP.

Letting go meant that I had to face my fears. In the hospital, we started calling it "risking," but what was really happening was my introduction to ERP (the "gold standard of treatment"), which consisted of exposing yourself to a given fear and refusing to respond to it. This treatment works for compulsions as well as obsessions as it disempowers the thought and/or behavior by experiencing the fear and finding that nothing happens. Yes, there is a short-term spike in anxiety. But long-term relief is lasting. For me, risking (or ERP) was all about letting go of control.

The approach that was taken with me was a combination of cognitive behavioral therapy (CBT), which helped me shift the dysfunctional OCD beliefs, and ERP, which helped me actively face my fears. I refer to this powerful approach as CBT/ERP. An antianxiety medication was prescribed, and it did help. But, in those early days of ERP, the anxiety would many times override the medication. The process was painful, both physically and emotionally. Anxiety ramped up to high anxiety and panic, finally receding into a lower level of anxiety, followed by limited relief. It was a long and exhausting process.

I was not in a locked psychiatric unit; I could have left at any time. But I was too afraid to leave, knowing that I would get worse if I did. It was also painful to see other patients, who had become trusted connections and friends, leave the unit. When new patients were admitted, I had to readjust to their energy, which could increase my anxiety.

My greatest fears had become germs, harming others, checking, and many other obsessional thoughts, such as, "Did I breathe on that person in group therapy, and will they get sick?" I often held my hand in front of my mouth as I was speaking (to protect others). And the group leaders would gently pull my hand back down in order to hear what I was saying. When the leader touched my hand, I would obsess about their germs and want to wash my hands. It was an endless, hideous loop.

If I walked down the hall, I would avoid touching anyone, with the obsession of contamination running in my head. Many nights, my head was under the covers, hiding from the germs. What if germs came under the door while I slept? What if I was going crazy?"

These obsessions slowly subsided with daily CBT/ERP. But I had to challenge all those thoughts by relearning how to trust others, myself, and life.

As we are often told, the patient is the last one to see progress. But I was, in fact, getting better. A crucial turning point came when my sense of humor returned. To me, finding humor in life was necessary for my survival. Losing my sense of humor, my ability to laugh, left a major hole in my spirit.

My sense of humor started to return one night when a health tech named Dennis, to whom I owe so much of my recovery, took me on a walk around the grounds of the hospital. I had not taken the risk to step outside at night in many weeks. I trusted Dennis, so it was easier for me to take that risk. I was not alone. We ended up at the parking lot where he showed me his 1972 Chevy, which was covered with what he called a "baby car blanket."

I burst out laughing. I had never heard of a baby car blanket. And somehow I found the very idea that a Chevy would need a baby blanket for protection to be hysterically funny. Why? Who knows? Who cares? All that mattered at that moment in time was that I was laughing again. And that release, that lightness of being that had been missing in my life for so long, felt nothing short of heaven. The normalcy of that singular experience, the gift of laughter that had long been a major part of my life, was my reintroduction to hope. And hope was everything. I knew that I was beginning to heal.

After I reclaimed laughter, I found another healing tool that I never knew was there: the ability to help and inspire others to help themselves. We would have two group therapy sessions per day in the TC-1 unit. My first days and weeks were about tears and coming clean, which then evolved into listening and investing in others. Many newcomers actually thought I was the leader of the group, which I wasn't. But, through service to others, I was not only helping them but was being helped in return. The mutual healing felt good.

In one of the therapy sessions, a man, whom I did not know well, was talking about his depression and how he worked with it. He said a very profound but simple bit of wisdom that I use to this day: "When I get up in the morning, and I am feeling depressed, I say one word to myself: 'walk.'"

Now, he wasn't talking about taking a walk; he was talking about taking one foot from under the covers and placing it on the floor, then placing his other foot on the floor, and then slowly taking one step at a time, until his mood started to shift. *Just walk.* Ever since then (from 1982 to today), I wake up and say, "Walk."

My whole life in recovery has been about taking steps— one step at a time, one foot in front of the other. Sometimes I take baby steps. But, in the big picture, it started with a willingness to take the first step, the willingness to move forward, and the willingness to trust that I could take a step like the man in the group session. That willingness did not come right away.

Trust that: If you are willing to "walk" and take one step at a time, you'll be on your way.

CHAPTER 2

The Power of Willingness and Trust

Nothing is easy to the unwilling.

~ Thomas Fuller

The opposite of fear is trust. It would take years of pain and struggle before I was willing to believe and trust that notion. As described in Chapter 1, I learned willingness the hard way when my severe OCD hit me like a ton of bricks. I hit bottom and that dissolved my resistance, allowing me to take my first step of healing: willingness and trust.

Throughout my childhood, teenage years, and into my 20s, I had always looked to my parents for answers. Whether about education, my living situation, money issues, or especially when I was sick, I continued to seek their advice and rely upon them for comfort, support, and a sense of relief.

Why was I so dependent on my parents for so much comfort and approval? Maybe insecurity? Maybe I needed their approval to validate my life decisions and my successes? Was it about overprotective conditioning? Codependency? Never individuating? More than likely, all of these were true: a dysfunctional pattern that affected how my adult years unfolded.

I was 29 and battling a severe case of OCD. I was washing my hands virtually all day, caught in checking rituals, especially when walking anywhere, and experiencing contamination phobias that drove me to spray Lysol on furniture for fear of germs. I was stuck in obsessional thinking that I could harm someone with just a thought. I didn't want to be touched and was unable to touch another person for fear of germs that might harm me or them. The worst of that fear came when I felt unable to hug my mother. The list of bizarre behaviors and fears seemed endless.

My family history and patterns led me to go to my mom and dad for the answers. Except going to my parents this time would be more difficult. It would mean that I would have to reveal the secret of my sexual addiction. And, already in such a severe state of obsession and compulsions, I felt that I was on the brink of losing my sanity. Going back to the apartment I shared with my girlfriend was no longer an option for, in addition to everything else I was battling, I was too filled with shame and guilt. I was lost.

I called my brother Dale, who was a psychologist in Seattle. He bluntly told me that I had three choices: check myself into a hospital, go to a hotel until I calmed down, or go to our mom and dad. In hindsight, I should have driven to the hospital and checked myself in. Instead, I chose the familiar path: my mom and dad. They had always known the answers. And I hoped they would have them again.

I took a deep breath and walked through their front door, pale and welling with tears. It was one of the most difficult moments in my life but, in looking back, perhaps one of the most courageous as well. Immediately, my mother knew I was terribly sick but had no idea to what extent.

After calming down to a level where I could talk, my father and I took a walk around the block. Now, my father was an extremely kind and sensitive man. But he was a quiet man too. I had this huge, heavy secret. And I was filled with shame and guilt. But I wanted to come clean and tell my father what had been going on in my life with my sex addiction. I could not get myself to say the words, as my embarrassment kept me stuck.

As we turned the corner and walked another block, my father said, in a gentle way, "I bet I can guess what's been going on with you."

In my wildest dreams, I could not imagine that my father would have any inkling of what I had been doing in my life for the previous 10 years, so I said, "I'll bet you a dollar that you can't guess."

He said, "I'll take that bet." He was quiet for just a moment and then added, "My best friend when I was a kid couldn't get enough sex. He talked about it. He was always with the girls. It was kind of a sexual addiction."

Even though I was in shame and pain, I felt a small smile come up and said, "I owe you a dollar." How my father intuitively and precisely knew continues to be a mystery to this day.

Over the next few months, my parents did everything they could to find me the best and most talented psychiatrist in our area, Phil Kavanaugh. I saw this man every day for weeks on end until the seriousness of my mental illness—OCD—was blatantly clear and not something my parents could deal with.

I will be forever grateful to my mother for finally making the courageous decision to ask Dr. Kavanaugh to admit me to a hospital, something my brother Dale had suggested I do from the very beginning. Frightened, but willing, I went to Dr. Kavanaugh's office. And he gently explained that the best place for me was in TC-1 at Good Samaritan Hospital in San Jose, the city I grew up in since age nine. I had visited TC-1 with my parents weeks before but was unwilling to go there. I knew I was very ill, but hospitalized in a psych ward? *No way!* That was for mentally ill people. Well, as the old slogan goes, "Denial isn't a river in Egypt." But now my psychiatrist, whom I had learned to trust, was telling me it was the right place.

Because of my fear of getting worse, and with the obsessions and compulsions escalating, I became *willing*. Pain is a great motivator. I was in hell, and TC-1 was a place that may have offered some ray of hope. To do the right thing for myself, I had to take a leap of faith—a leap of trust.

Dr. Kavanaugh, whom I was now calling Phil, had gained my trust and actually drove me to the hospital a few blocks from his office. I remember walking down a long hallway. At the end were two brown, double doors that led into TC-1.

We walked side by side down the hall. And, about halfway down, I looked over at Phil and asked, "Do you really think I belong here?"

Phil smiled. "It's the right thing, Jim."

He always did his best to take the drama out of any situation. He admitted me. And I remember overhearing him say to the staff tech that I would be staying for a longer period than others. Of course, this scared me. But I simply had to trust Phil. Somewhere deep inside, I must have known that this would save my life.

I sat in my room as the intake tech took my information. I remember feeling a sense of both relief and comfort that something positive was finally happening to help the devastating emotional and physical pain of OCD. She listened to my story, took some notes, let me cry, and then calmly and quietly left. I sat on the bed, alone and exhausted, not knowing what would follow. I waited for a doctor, a psych tech, anyone to tell me what was next. Time passed, and eventually I had to go to the bathroom—one of my major germ phobias.

There was a mix-up with the private rooms. And I was displaced for a while, meaning that I had no choice but to use the public bathroom in the psych unit. A public bathroom in a hospital! *Are you kidding me?* Talk about fear. I was mortified. My anxiety shot through the roof, and I panicked. I spent three hours in that bathroom in a cold sweat, washing my hands over and over again. As I always did, I put on a face of normalcy for those coming in and leaving. But I was alone in a psych ward bathroom with horrifying OCD fears of germs and contamination. I was physically and emotionally spent but could not leave. I was stuck in rituals. Three hours had passed, and no one had come to check on me. Were they abandoning me? Were they testing me? Did they know that I was struggling? Did they know that I was immobilized in terror?

Shaking, with sweat running down my face, I finally forced myself out the bathroom door, not touching the doorknob with my hand. I must have just slipped out as someone was coming in. During the time I was in the bathroom, I had missed dinner. I was furious that no one seemed to care. Anger temporarily distracted my OCD fears, and I called my parents and Phil.

Later that night, the staff prepared a tray of food for me. Eating and complaining, I sat with my parents and Phil in the psych ward dining room. In his usual gentle way, Phil explained how things worked. There were rules in the ward.

And they did not bend for me. But what I think he was really doing was introducing me to the fact that I had to work too. There were no free rides. No one was going to save me. And that pissed me off even more. I wanted a quick fix. Where was the magic doctor who was going to heal me?

That was the first of my many days of kicking and screaming about one word: willingness.

I had to be *willing to feel* the depths of pain, every bit of it, before I could feel any semblance of relief. Although it sounds cruel, it was the truth. And the only way for the recovery process to begin. I had to *trust* the process, a new process that was foreign to me.

The staff did not stage my bathroom incident. It was part of my process of healing. You cannot get to recovery by resistance. Willingness to go to the hospital was nothing compared to the steps I would have to take to start the process of healing. I had to be willing to go through all of these fears that were seemingly out of my control.

The first days in TC-1 were the toughest and by far the most important of my stay. I had to become willing to let go of trying to control the OCD and trust that there was a better way. Let me say that again: *I had to become willing to let go of control and trust that there was a better way to heal.*

This was a powerful lesson in healing my broken spirit: *willingness.*

I had to ask myself, "How willing am I to take on OCD? How willing am I to face my fears? How willing am I to hear the words that would help me heal myself? How willing am I to take medication? How willing am I to participate in the therapies of ERP and CBT? How willing am I to go to daily group therapy sessions and listen to others? How willing am I"—and this was the most crucial—"to come out of the closet and let others know my sexual addiction secrets that eventually triggered OCD? How willing am I to trust that all of this would help me?"

I took the risk the first night to tell my story to the group. In tears, I told a true story of my self-defeating sexual addiction, losing everything I loved, and now being stuck in this strange disorder called OCD. As I wept, no one criticized or shamed me. I felt that, in some way, the group understood and maybe even empathized. Something shifted that night. It was a shift towards my journey to willingness and trust. However, it would be some time before I deeply understood the healing power of those two words.

Trust that: My resistance to be willing and trust was the OCD saying, "My way or no way." I have learned, with time, that I had to be willing to take the risk to trust others. I had to let others in; I couldn't do this alone.

CHAPTER 3

Surrender

*All our reasoning ends in
surrender to feeling.*

~ Blaise Pascal

As the weeks went by in TC-1, I was waiting for someone to come through those big, brown double doors and save me. Who that would be, I did not know. How they would save me, I had no idea. When would they come? They never did.

I was about to have a lesson in *surrendering*. Before I could really commit to working on resisting the compulsions and obsessions, I had to be willing to accept the fact that the *only* person who could heal me was me. And I had to surrender to my feelings—something I had never fully done before. The notion was difficult to accept or even think about.

So how did I consciously go about surrendering to feeling my fears? In a cynical and judgmental way, it started with some simple observations in the unit ... and asking myself some very hard questions.

I remember watching a family that was visiting a patient in the corner of the main living area of the psych ward. The family rallied around their loved one. A young girl in the family was playing on a chair, and she slipped and fell. She may have sprained her leg. But it seemed more than likely that she was uninjured from the fall. What was shocking to me was the amount of attention paid to the girl. Obviously concerned, psych techs urgently ran over to check on her.

My inner voice screamed, "What about *me*? Do I have to fall off a chair to get some *attention* around here?" In that moment, I thought, "If it's physical, you get attention; if it's mental, you're left behind. Alone."

The little girl falling and the attention she received were appropriate for that moment. The attention one receives when suffering from a disorder such as OCD is far trickier because the illness requires a different kind of attention.

In Chapter 2, I talked about being stuck for hours in the psych ward bathroom on the day I was admitted. In looking back, if someone had come into the bathroom where I had been stuck in rituals and had dragged me out, would it have truly helped me or kept me in a place of dependency?

Before the hospital, I was extremely dependent on my parents to take care of my OCD. They unknowingly helped me into helplessness. At home, there was always someone to validate my fears. I would take showers and use up to a dozen towels to dry off for fear of contamination. My mother would wash the towels for me. It was as if she and my father were unconsciously enabling me in their attempt to protect me from further anxiety and panic. It didn't work.

At this point, I must make it clear that abandoning, or forcing a person into actions that create horrific feelings or fear, is not the answer either. In my opinion, "tough love" does not work. It's a matter of something else. And that something else is *surrender*.

Now, you may bristle at the word "surrender" because we are taught by our teachers, parents, and culture to "fight, fight, fight." However, I learned another way to heal without the exhausting fight. I'm asking you to take a leap of faith and look at the word "surrender" in a different context—a context that is a tool for relief.

Surrendering to Anxiety

I needed to take my surrendering in two parts. I first learned how to surrender to the anxiety. Yes, *surrender to the anxiety*, for it was and still is the most acute issue I deal with day to day. Then I needed to learn how to surrender to the disorder itself, to find acceptance and some level of peace. Both brought me a sense of relief and a sense of moving forward rather than being crippled by my fears.

Let's start with anxiety that OCD creates. I have found that it's almost impossible to contemplate any decision or choice about acceptance when feeling anxious. In other words, "Don't ask me to make a decision when I'm having a panic attack!"

I started to realize that OCD loves a good fight. But OCD always seemed to be winning. My anxiety was consistent and predictable and would operate almost the same way every time. I would have a life stressor or fear, which would trigger an obsession or a phobia, which, in turn, would trigger a compulsion or ritual (usually hand-washing, counting, or checking—all of which I despised). The compulsions were horrendous and would last for hours, as I have mentioned. But, as dysfunctional as they seemed, they did focus my attention. And the anxiety lessened until the next feeling of fear sprang up again. It was a vicious cycle.

So, with help, I took a hard look at this thing called "anxiety" and what I call its "true nature." I learned that the nature of anxiety involves *resistance* and *control*. Whenever I felt out of control, I felt a feeling of anxiety. Whether or not I was out of control in my life, the feeling was real. When I resisted doing something that I knew in my heart was the best for me but would be difficult to do, I experienced that feeling of anxiety again. The best example for my feeling of resistance was when I first visited the hospital where I knew I should have gone in the first place.

My parents had taken me there just to have a look. Even though it looked nothing like a psychiatric unit in the movies—no *Cuckoo's Nest* there—I was still fearful and resistant, even though I knew on a very deep level that I should be there to get the help I needed. After that visit, my feeling of anxiety ramped up to the maximum. Could it be that if the true nature of anxiety is control and resistance, then the true nature of peace is letting go of control and resistance?

Phil encouraged me to let go and surrender. He promised me that, if I let go of control, I would *gain* control—a paradox that I much later found to be true and healing. But what was I letting go of? I was letting go of trying to control my feelings. I was encouraged daily to *feel the feelings and do nothing.* And the feelings of fear and anxiety would dissipate by themselves. After practicing feeling the feelings and doing nothing, I found that the anxiety only slowed down. It didn't go away. What was I doing wrong?

It wasn't that I was doing anything wrong. But I was impatient. For most of us, "feeling your feelings" is not something we learned when growing up and takes practice. Surrendering to my feelings, acknowledging my feelings, owning my feelings, letting go of controlling my feelings, and being in a state of nonresistance and replacing it with acceptance were not concepts heard, taught, or encouraged in school. But now I was in a school for my very survival, salvaging my life—a better life—and I had to put my trust in Phil.

OCD had robbed me of trusting myself.

Letting Go of Control to Get Control

Phil told me that the objective was to let go of control in order to get control and to let go of my resistance to feeling my feelings.

I had to address anxiety in this way: "Hey, I recognize you. You're that familiar feeling of anxiety that seems to want to control me. Well, have at it. Bat me around. I surrender. And I refuse to fight."

At this point, you may be raising your eyebrows and saying, "Refuse to fight? *What?* Refuse to obsess, worry, or wash my hands or some other compulsion? But the urge is so great!"

I never said this was easy. But I do know from experience that it is one of the most powerful and effective ways to peace. I know this may sound odd or strange, but the paradox was clear: By surrendering to my feelings and not following the obsessions or compulsions, I was resisting the urge. It does take a powerful and courageous will to surrender.

These days, when one of those bizarre obsessions pops into my mind—"You could harm someone by thinking that thought" or "If you don't say you're sorry now, you will be abandoned"—I surrender by saying back to the OCD obsession, "Thanks for sharing. I'm not caring."

Surrendering and having feelings rather than acting on them was my resistance to OCD and still is.

I remember when Phil, after validating my fears for some time, finally challenged me to have the anxiety bat me around. I was scared to death.

"No way," I said. "I have to fight this thing. And you have to validate everything I'm fighting for."

He just smiled, as he always did, and said, "Just breathe into the feelings."

I thought, "What the hell *is* this? Is he abandoning me? Breathe into *what*?"

I was kicking and screaming in my mind. I wanted some validation, some magic words that would take the anxiety away. But Phil just sat with me, encouraged me to just be with it, and not to fight it or control it. Just feel it. Be with it.

How did I feel? I was pissed! What was he springing on me? Just *feel* it? What was he *talking* about? This hurts!

"Feel all of your feelings, even the painful ones right now, Jim," he said. "Trust me. Just be with the feeling of anxiety, and it will go away. There is no way over it. There is no way around it. You have to go *through* it. Feel it, and it will gradually go away."

And so, with an ounce of trust, I felt the feeling and did nothing.

It took less than an hour before the anxious feeling started to subside. The anxiety was going away, and I was doing it on my own. Little did I know then that he was teaching me how to surrender to my feelings. And, for the first time in my life, I was really feeling my feelings. And I felt in control.

This is a paradox. Don't get me wrong here. You are not suddenly cured from OCD because you are surrendering to and feeling your feelings. This has been part of my recovery process. I have to work hard at resisting compulsions and obsessions much of the time. For example, when I am in the shower and OCD is screaming at me to wash some part of my body one more time, I work hard to follow my ERP coach's guidance to wash only once. Believe me, that's damn hard. And it is work. But it's worth it.

Feel the Feelings

These are words that I live by to this day.

At this point, you may be saying, "But anxiety hurts. It's painful, and I have to do something. I have to fight!"

Yes, you do. And the fight is paradoxically about surrender. Isn't that strange? But it's true.

Naturally, use any and all tools to lessen the severity of acute anxiety. I use a variety of refocusing tools. I exercise. I meditate, using a guided imagery breathing meditation. I play piano, watch TV, get on the computer, listen to music, or get out in nature and take a walk. I try to refocus and place my attention on anything that looks and feels peaceful because imagery can shift the brain pathways into balance.

A key to healing is to surrender to the feelings. Feel the feelings, and let them pass through. They will always pass through. Feelings are nothing more than energy. And, as all energy is in motion, fluid, it will move someplace else if we allow it and get out of the way.

Anxiety will always leave if you don't put up a fight. If you resist having the feeling rather than going through the feeling, you are playing a game called "resistance." The more you resist, the more it persists. By refusing to play the anxiety game of resistance, and instead use the recovery tool of surrendering and feeling the feelings, you can reset your brain to a place of empowerment rather than disempowerment. I work with this concept every day of my life.

Surrendering to What Is

The second part of surrendering came in the form of surrendering to having the disorder. It had nothing to do with giving up or not accepting healing for the disorder itself. It was more of a "coming-out-of-denial mentality" and truly understanding OCD for what it is.

During the first weeks of my hospital stay, I felt alone and out of control and wondered if I had lost my mind. I remember looking out the window of my hospital room to an open field and thinking, "I am trapped in this psychiatric ward, and just beyond that window is life. Will I ever get out there again?"

There was a running track around the hospital for staff. They would pass my window, looking healthy and fit as I was on my eighth hour of washing my hands. I felt isolated and disconnected with lots of fear. Those bright, sunny days for the runners outside of my window were dark, hopeless days inside my small room. I had bottomed out.

That's when the denial stopped and the healing began. I had to come to a place where I could look at myself in the mirror, cry, grieve, and eventually surrender to the fact that I had a neurobiological disorder—a mental illness called OCD.

After I had finally and fully surrendered to and accepted the fact that I had OCD—just like the approximately one in 40 adults and one in 100 children in this country alone—the good news began to follow. *I could be treated!* Fortunately for those of us who suffer from the pain of OCD, it is a treatable disorder. I was increasingly willing to feel the feelings, knowing they would not persist if I did not resist them. I came to trust this simple yet powerful concept and tool and use it daily. I know it's hard. But, with practice, it's doable.

A final thought about resistance versus surrendering and acceptance because they are key to recovery. I always remind myself that, if I had diabetes, high blood pressure, cancer, or heart disease, would I be so reluctant to take medication or alternative treatments? Would I be resistant to surrendering to the fact that I have an illness that could be treated?

My inner thoughts always respond, "Hell, no! I'd do anything to help myself recover from those diseases."

The only differences between OCD and other illnesses are where the biology resides, how it affects your life, and how it is treated.

As I daily encourage myself, I also send that spirit of encouragement to you to come out of denial or the stubborn belief that you can deal with OCD alone. I had to step away from the misconception that I could handle OCD with just willpower.

When you come to accept that you have OCD, and commit to recovery, I encourage you to go to the highest mountain and scream, "I have OCD. And I choose recovery over this!"

I did. Well, maybe not on a mountaintop. But whatever it took to surrender, then *and only then* did I become open to the path of least resistance. The healing gates began to open ... and still are.

Trust that: Trust and practice feeling your feelings, feeling the anxiety rather than moving towards rituals, feeling the obsessional thoughts and identifying them as OCD—minute by minute, hour by hour, day by day—and you will feel a gradual peace come to you. When it does, you'll remember it because it feels so good.

CHAPTER 4

Pain Forced Me to Change

One cannot get through life without pain. What we can do is choose how to use the pain life presents to us.

~ Bernie S. Siegel

Pain was one of my greatest teachers. Pain forced me to *be willing to change*. The excruciating pain of OCD brought humility into my life. My hurt, my pain, was so profound that my psychiatrist told me it was the worst case of OCD he had ever seen, which made me feel all the more horrified.

"Oh, great! What am I supposed to do with *that*?" I wondered.

Later, that same man helped me save my own life.

I wouldn't let anyone touch me. I would wash my hands up to nine hours a day, which in turn made my hands dry, red, and raw. I had germ and contamination phobias to the point where I believed that dangerous germs were sneaking under the door of my room at TC-1 to attack me while I slept, thus leading to very little sleep for weeks on end. I would hold the covers over my head, thinking that they would protect me from these dangerous germs. Yet, throughout these obsessions and compulsions, I kept thinking, "This is crazy ... but what if it's *true*?"

Each night in TC-1, I would finish two to three hours of evening rituals, many times asking a night tech to observe me as I no longer trusted what I was doing; that is, my OCD mind did not trust that I was washing my hands correctly, or brushing my teeth correctly, or using the towel correctly, or getting into bed correctly. You name it. Nothing felt right. OCD had robbed me of my own trust and of my memory of how to function. It was replaced with irrational fears that I was doing something wrong. And these mistakes would eventually hurt me or someone else if I didn't do them correctly. It was an illogical, painful loop.

I talked to people with my hands covering my mouth for fear that my germs may be spread to them. I spent hours on the toilet, straining to void everything "toxic" by using several rolls of toilet paper for fear of germs and contamination. My "magical," irrational thoughts included fears of harming others, especially family members, and counting rituals that specifically avoided the number six.

Now, let me first be clear about this harming thing. Phil taught me a term called "jumping germs" as applied to OCD. It went like this: I felt that germs could literally jump from any source—to me, to another person—and in some way harm that person. The result was guilt and shame. And again it was all my fault. All of these fears and countless others caused tremendous anxiety and physical pain through the course of each day.

Next, I want to expand a bit about an obsession that lasted for many years: the obsession about the number six. Many people challenged with OCD have number obsessions. The number six was mine. Why the number six? I had no formal religious training or biblical reference to believe that the number six represented some form of evil power, or any power at all. I remember seeing a horror film that talked about the devil and the number six. A *movie*—nothing based in any reality! But the power of that film scripted a fear in my mind until years later, when a trusted friend clued me in on the generally accepted historical meaning around the number six, which had absolutely nothing to do with devils or evil. Putting my trust in one friend who offered me the facts was enough. I was able to let it go. I later learned that

(sometimes you just have to borrow someone else's brain for a while until you can trust your own.)

Walking down the hospital halls at TC-1, I was compelled to avoid people and to constantly look over my shoulder to make sure I hadn't walked near or on anything that I construed as dirty or contaminated. Even the simple task of tying my shoes took hours for fear of not doing it in a "germ-proof way." I had to be very careful about those "magical germs" that might be on my shoes and transferred to my hands. Every morning, I would pound my shoes on the floor repeatedly, with the intent to rid them from the magical germs before I actually put them on my feet.

One morning, another patient came to my door and asked, "Would you stop pounding? I am trying to sleep."

He wasn't enraged, angry, or livid. But that singular request seemed to pull me back into the present, and I stopped the pounding and put on my shoes. My brain shifted away from the OCD, away from me, to a place of compassion for him. I experienced a glimmer of light amidst the pain.

But the momentum of OCD continued. I was consumed with overwhelming guilt. I obsessed on anything that I could remember doing or saying to anyone in the past or present that may have offended them in any fashion. I had it all. And I was a mess. I was phobic about people, places, and things. The OCD made my world smaller and smaller every day. I went to bed exhausted and in pain from constant obsessions and rituals and woke up crying, knowing it would start all over again.

I was not suicidal. But I was praying for God to take me: "Please take me away from this pain."

I had hit rock bottom. Strangely, I was completely cognizant that my fears and phobias couldn't be real because I saw others in the psych unit sharing food, hugging each other, washing their hands once, and walking away from the sink. The world just didn't operate in the way I was thinking.

Later, my wonderful CBT therapist Ron told me, "If the world operated the way you think it does, we'd all be dead."

That statement was honest and direct. And I found that I needed such directness and a good dose of humor from a person in order to *trust* at the deepest level. Trust came to be the core issue of my healing. OCD seemingly had robbed me of trust. I didn't trust my own thoughts. Sound familiar?

Bottom line: I had a wounded spirit and a wounded belief system. I was in emotional and physical pain. And I trusted no one—especially myself. What was I supposed to do with that wonderful scenario?

The overwhelming pain forced me into willingness to try, one minute at a time. I mean, seriously, at rock bottom, I had no choice. Pain is a great motivator. Like many of us, I took pain to the unbearable brink before being willing to change.

To lessen my pain, I had to push through the fear, be less resistant, and do the work. Let me repeat that: *I had to do the work*. I had to be willing to really trust Phil, and let in his words, his prescribed medicines, and treatments. I had to be willing to take the risk to face the fears. And, let me make this clear: *None of it was easy*.

Trust that: OCD comes with pain. That's just a fact about the disorder. However, I don't think anyone has to bottom out and go as deep into pain as I did to start the work. Take a step now, even if it is the tiniest baby step. At least you'll be on the right path.

CHAPTER 5

Letting Go of Control: The Power of Popcorn

Beliefs create reality.

~ Melody Beattie

As I made a few friends in the hospital, I was told that I was doing better, even though I wasn't aware of my own progress.

Late one evening, I found myself with a few people in the living room of TC-1, surrounding a large bowl of popcorn. I was relaxed. And I was connecting with people. Although I was aware that I felt less anxious, I wasn't about to touch that bowl of popcorn. Everyone's hands were in the bowl—for me, an absolute OCD nightmare! I just sat there and watched. Most of the people knew me for my sense of humor, which was coming back. And they embraced my personality, not the OCD.

I vividly remember the coziness and comfort of hanging out with like-minded people, just sitting around, eating popcorn, and how, at that moment, my fear was slowly turning to trust. However, was I trusting enough to—for the first time in weeks—let go and touch food that others had their hands in? This went against all of my obsessions and fears of germs and contamination and harming others. The OCD warned me that, if I touched the popcorn and had any germs on my hands, then someone else who grabbed a handful that I had contaminated could become sick or maybe even die.

At that moment, my trusting mind said, "Now wait a minute, Jim. Are you seeing anyone dropping over and dying in this group? You used to do this as a kid with your family. Take the risk."

I think the others sensed that I was on the verge of letting go of control and taking that monumental risk. I could feel it. Some even gently encouraged me.

"Go ahead, Jim," they offered. "Nothing is going to happen."

There is nothing more nurturing in this world than being with people who believe in you. Armed with that trust, I paused for a moment and ever so slowly put my hand in the bowl, surgically removing one small piece of popcorn, and ate it. They all smiled and went on talking. I felt as though I had just reached the top of the mountain. And, empowered, I tried it again. What did I feel at that moment? The only word is "freedom." Believe me, it tasted really good! By the end of the evening, I was able to take a handful of popcorn and eat it. I felt alive again.

As the wonderful Susan Jeffers reminds us in the title of her book, *Feel the Fear ... and Do It Anyway,* that night I did it anyway by letting go of control, trusting others, and, in turn, trusting myself. This was the first of many breakthroughs in letting go of trying to control my fears.

A more "alone breakthrough" came while standing in front of a linen closet. Remember, at that time, most of my fears were based around germs and contamination. In TC-1, they wanted us to do as much for ourselves as possible. That was perhaps one of the hardest parts of being in a psych ward. Talk was available. But, when it came to *doing*, you were on your own much of the time, including getting your own towels and sheets stored in the main closet for the entire ward.

As you can imagine, this was a big challenge for me due to my extreme germ phobia. I thought, "How many people touched these towels? What sheets were touched by others and then put back in the closet for some reason?" My mind went on an obsessive fear ride, which paralyzed me, as I opened the two doors of that huge and ominous closet. I must have stood there for three hours.

I noticed that several of the techs who knew me and knew of my *risking* process were hanging around. They were not helping me or offering to help but rather waiting to see if I would take a set of towels and sheets that I desperately needed. Remember too that I was still in a hand-washing ritual most of my days.

So, there I stood, looking at all these white hand towels and white sheets. I started to sweat, which always meant to me that my anxiety was ramping up. But I was determined. One hour went by, then two. I tried to reach out and touch but just as quickly retracted because the fear was overwhelming. Now there were more techs watching from afar but acting as if they were preoccupied.

"A little help?" I asked softly. But no one responded.

I believe they knew I was ready to take the risk. Sweat dripped down my face. I was a mess but couldn't seem to move from that spot. Something was about to happen, and part of me knew it. Finally, I quickly grabbed 10 towels and two sets of sheets and dashed for my room. I placed them on my counter and sat on my bed. I felt like I had just ended a marathon of emotion, crossing the finish line with an armload of towels. The techs said nothing to me about my success. But I knew they were talking to each other about my progress.

It was a painful risk. Painful and hard to let go of control in order to gain control. But, you know, that's how it goes for most of us. When we challenge our fears, pain comes before the letting go. But it's always worth it. I haven't stopped working on letting go since.

The Steps

After I was released from the hospital, my control issues were better. But I wanted to learn more about how they affected my life as a whole and how to better deal with them. How do I stop being a "controller"?

The answer came in a form that was not so easy to swallow. And, quite frankly, it irritated the hell out of me. I was advised by my main guide Phil to try a 12-step program in addition to everything else I was doing, including CBT, ERP, and medication.

"What?" I asked with my usual resistance. "A 12-step program? I'm not an alcoholic or a drug addict."

Phil smiled and said, "Just trust me, Jim. You're bright enough to take that first step of the 12 steps and fill in the blank, aren't you? It goes, 'I am powerless over _____, and my life has become unmanageable.'"

Instead of "alcohol" or "the alcoholic" or "cocaine" or any number of descriptions that go into that blank, depending on the 12-step program you attend, I filled in the blank with "anxiety" I started with the Al-Anon 12-step group as there were no Obsessive Compulsive Anonymous 12-step programs at the time. I filled in the blank with "anxiety." But "OCD" or "fear" would do.

At first, I was resistant to hearing all the problems and slogans that came with any 12-step meeting. Phil encouraged me to just stay with it and to talk. I did.

And, after some time, the wisdom, comfort, and connection started to filter in. There, I learned how to look at control issues from a spiritual perspective. This was not a religious perspective at all but one based in developing my intuitive spirit, which was lost with the onset of OCD. It was a reclaiming of my wounded spirit. And, believe me, a wounded spirit takes time and gentle hands to fix.

Slogans came from those meetings that, in my earlier years, sounded like Hallmark cards: "Progress not perfection," "One day at a time," "Turn it over," "What others think of you is none of your business," "Fake it until you make it," and (my favorite) "Let go and let God."

"Wait a minute! I thought this was not a religious program."

It's not. The use of the words "God" or "higher power" are intended to mean something outside of yourself and, in my opinion, inside of you at the same time. Some people make the meeting their higher power. Not a bad idea. The collective wisdom of those people is bigger than I am. And yet I am a part of it at the same time. Some make their higher power the ocean. Also a great image for it is outside of us. And, as we are about 65% water ourselves and can't survive without it, that connection can be a powerful one. Nature is a good one too. As I heard long ago, "To find your nature, get into nature." Still, some make and call their higher power God, whatever that means for them. It is up to the individual. It is a choice.

What matters most is that you believe in something more than your fears—something bigger than you that you can connect with. So, once I got past the "God" thing,

I really wanted to understand the slogan, "Let go and let God." What did that mean? What did it have to do with my control issues?

The "G" Word

"Let go and let God." *Oh, no.* The "G" word! I heard it over and over again. I heard it from all kinds of self-help, inspirational experts: Dr. Wayne Dyer, Melody Beattie, Marianne Williamson, Dr. Deepak Chopra, and my psychiatrist Dr. Phil Kavanaugh. Everyone I respected was using that phrase and that word in one way or another. Again, what did it mean in relation to control, OCD, and me?

Finally, I cornered Phil.

He sat back in his chair and quietly said, "Jim, you're making too much of this. 'Let go and let God' means stop trying to figure it out."

Well, that stopped me firmly in my tracks! Challenged by OCD, I was trying to figure out all of my fears. "What did they mean? Were they real? How would I negotiate with them?" Okay, so I got that part of the slogan: "Let go of trying to control every detail of my life, and let life happen," meaning "Let go of being in a constant state of trying to figure everything out."

Now what about the "God" part?

Phil simply replied, "Oh. The 'God' thing. Well, don't get hung up on that, Jim. You know we are all part of the universe—part of God, if you want to use that term. If that bothers you, use the word 'source.' That works too."

Phil grinned out of respect, for he knew that I could handle the concept that we are connected to something, something bigger than ourselves. The name wasn't as important as the idea that we did come from *something*. And that something is still around. We're not alone.

He looked at me directly and wrapped it up. "So, I'm telling you that the way to stop the controlling is to stop trying to figure it out—whatever 'it' is in your life—and turn it over to the universe. The 'universe' or 'source' or 'God,' whatever you want to call it, has a much better handle on things. Don't ya think?" He smiled and sent me on my way.

I was left with all of this spiritual wisdom that seemed easy enough to comprehend. But how was I going to put it into action? I reminded myself of what I learned in surrendering: "If I let go of control and just feel the feelings, they will dissipate because all feelings are energy. And all energy goes somewhere else if you don't fight it." Basically, it was about getting out of my own way. So, there I was, feeling my feelings and doing my best not to ritualize or obsess.

I allowed myself to feel it all, and I took no action. Let go of control. It was not easy. And it took a lot of practice. Many times I needed outside help, whether it was Phil's help or help with expressing my frustration, fear, and anger at meetings. Some days were just spent sweating through it. And, to this day, as I continue this practice, at times I still forget the process and must lean on others to remind me to feel my feelings and let go.

Ah ha! So that's what the slogan "progress not perfection" means. There are some days where amazing things happen with the OCD fears and in all aspects of my life. The less "perfection" I put into letting go of control, the more "progress" I made toward being in control. It felt good. And feeling good was a feeling I hadn't experienced for a long time—feeling good by letting go of control and handing it to the universe.

For many years, I thought of this as such a strange or foreign concept. But it worked. It worked with OCD compulsions and obsessions. It worked with calming down from anxiety. It worked with any external and internal conflicts, such as worrying about things like money and relationships. Literally, all aspects of life and living could be managed, or at least made easier, by acknowledging and practicing the concept, "Let go and let God."

I still struggle a bit with the "let God" part. But I have come up with a way to soothe my struggle that works for me. And it may work for you too. The formula is as follows: If "God" doesn't work for you, try a word that represents it: "peace," "nature," "serenity," "connection," "abundance," "soothing," "gratitude," "appreciation," or "love." In my ongoing recovery from OCD, I will gladly embrace any of these wonderful words and feelings. Wouldn't you?

Phil always told me that it was about "believing." If I wasn't ready to truly believe, I faked it until I made it. In letting go of control, I gained a feeling of control. In letting "God," "my higher self," "the universe," or "source" handle it, I was truly operating in what Phil called "spiritual gear." Reclaiming my spirit that the disorder took away was now my hope. "Spiritual gear" is a good place to be.

Trust that: There's a paradox here that you need to trust. When you let go of control, you get control. Plain, simple, not so easy—but really true.

CHAPTER 6

Living on My Own

The only way to get what you really want is to let go of what you don't want.

~ Iyanla Vanzant

After spending six weeks in TC-1, including Christmas and New Year's, Phil told me that I was ready to take a shot at living on my own. But he would not release me from the unit until I found an apartment and signed a rental agreement. That was the deal. Note that I was not in a locked psych ward. TC-1 was a unit where people could come and go. However, if their doctor determined that they were not ready to go out into the world, it was called AMA (Against Medical Advice). I trusted Phil implicitly. And I wasn't about to walk out of any door AMA.

With the help and support of my wonderful Uncle Richard, I was able to search for an apartment. He would take time during the day to drive me around. This was a risk in itself. Going into strange apartments triggered a myriad of contamination fears connected to the occupants of each apartment.

"Who are these people? Are there germs in their apartments that could contaminate my uncle or me?"

The higher good forced the "risking tool" to take over; that is, I truly wanted and was determined to get my life back and be independent once again. That was the higher good. When the higher good is high enough, I found that I was willing to risk more—risk feeling my fears and pushing through them anyway.

For many reasons, it was a long process of searching for the right apartment: location, visualizing myself in the space, and of course price. Finally, I did something that I continue to do to this day: *I made a decision and called whatever I hit "the target."* Phil shared that slogan, and that's exactly what I was doing. I chose an apartment out of many and made it okay. Let me say that again: *I made a decision, and I made it okay.* Was the apartment perfect? No. But I didn't need perfect. I needed to make a decision, which was a step forward. I made the decision to make it good enough for me at that moment in time. I visualized fixing it up. In my mind's eye, I saw where my furniture would go, where the pictures would be hung, where my small television would sit, my desk, my bed. And the apartment—the *target of my decision*—started to look good. I could see it.

I had learned another great tool: If I could make a decision and visualize it as "good enough for now," my anxiety lessened and creativity bloomed. I found that, when creativity entered my spirit, I reconnected with something that felt very hopeful, healing, and nurturing. I never wanted to let go of it. It was similar to the early weeks in the hospital when I was unable to touch anyone. I became touch starved. I remember the first time I took the risk of shaking Phil's hand goodbye after our daily visit, and how I didn't want to let go. I simply didn't want to let go of the man's hand. At that moment, his hand represented that creative spirit: warm, hopeful, healing, loving, comforting, and a feeling of coming home.

The Attempt to Quiet the Mind

Before I moved into my new apartment, there was a three-week waiting period because the apartment needed some repair. I moved back into my parents' house. While I was welcomed, I knew they were not thrilled and more than likely had many concerns:

"Would all the tools he learned in the hospital fade away? Would he go back to using a dozen towels to take a two-hour shower? Would he be asking for reassurance just to get out of the bathroom?"

I'm sure these questions raced though my parents' minds. At this time, however, I did have new tools that I had learned in the hospital and was damned if I was going to let go of them. I was also going to a daily outpatient therapy group. But what was I to do with my time in between therapy and my personal psychiatry visits? I knew that CBT/ERP was the answer for me. But the thought was frightening because, this time around, I was on my own.

One night, I took the risk. I decided to take myself out on a date. Yep, I took myself to a movie. *Tootsie* with Dustin Hoffman had just come out, and I was dying to see it. But it meant challenging my fears. I knew I could drive myself to the theater and that would be okay. But buying tickets? Would the kid at the box office have germs on his hands and therefore the ticket be contaminated? That was the first cognitive battle. You don't get sick from germs on tickets. If that were true in the real world, I would see a theater full of ill people. Sounds silly. But I had to think this way to get through the blockade of dark, magical thinking and fears.

Next was the big one: I had to go into the movie theater and find a seat that didn't look or feel like it was covered with contamination or some other nasty, magical thing that could hurt me. If I could tackle that, the next battle would be to sit down among strangers ... a lot of strangers. The place was jammed. It was opening night!

So, there I sat in the center of the last row, wedged between two middle-aged people, who were there not to take an OCD risk but to enjoy a movie. I crossed my legs, cocooned up and frozen in the same position for two hours, feeling claustrophobic. I would feel a nudge here, an arm touch there, a coat rub across my arm. And all the while they laughed at Dustin Hoffman's adventures as Dorothy Michaels.

I tried to focus on watching the film. But my mind was preoccupied with avoiding the touch of the people on either side of me. If you took that scenario and added a germ phobia to it, that would give you a taste of what I was feeling. Yet, I knew I could get through it. I was using all of my tools, even while the sweat ran down my forehead.

The movie finally ended. I think I may have seen 10% of the film. The credits rolled. And I was the first one out of the theater.

The lesson, and the win, was that I felt the fear and took the risk anyway. It was a huge exposure experience for me. But most of all it introduced me to socialization rather than isolation. To practice this, I went to more and more movies. A place that had once felt safe growing up as a movie buff— with my father being an educational film director and his influence—now took on a whole new meaning. Movie theaters went from an exposure challenge to a sanctuary of distraction. The movie theater became a tool to quiet my mind. All of this helped my re-entry into life.

The Obsessive Committee

How could I attempt to quiet an obsessive mind? I call it "the obsessive committee"—a committee that always seemed to be on duty; a doubting committee that would challenge every move or thought I had. What could I do to shut down that committee just for a moment or two?

Church.

"*What?* Church?"

I'm a nonpracticing, nice Jewish boy from Wisconsin. I rarely go to temple, let alone go to church. Well, at that time, I was alone—kind of. It was the OCD and me. Besides taking myself to movies, I found that walking on a college campus felt soothing. I lived near the large university campus of Stanford. And, at this time, the students were on spring break.

I walked into the magnificent church in the center of the campus and just sat there. Now, I was lucky that the symptom of scrupulosity was not part of my lineup of fears, or I may have started obsessing on some moral or religious thought. Instead, I just looked at the art. There was no charge or fear lurking behind what the symbols meant, for they held no significance for me. However, I was able to focus on the stained glass, the brilliant colors, the statues, and the entirety of the atmosphere that the church offered.

I also cried. I felt sorry for myself. And, although I experienced a handful of OCD fears, they always seemed to sweep over me as I was leaving, not coming. I knew that I was going to a place that would soothe me. And it did soothe me, sitting in that church. Upon leaving, stepping outside of the refuge of diversion, I knew that I was going back to my familiar regiment of fears. I was determined, however, to meet the challenge of taking a risk, allowing myself to feel good about it, and continuing that feeling of empowerment as I headed home, knowing that I was indeed making progress. But none of it was easy.

Strangely enough, while I sat in that church, I let myself have a conversation with what I call "God." Don't get me wrong here. I didn't need to go to the church at Stanford to connect with my higher power. But it felt like a good time and a peaceful place to ask a few questions. The answers came later in my recovery.

In those early days, the Stanford church had two concrete healing purposes: It was a place to go rather than isolate at home. And it quieted my mind for a short while. I now know that the energy of a quiet place—whether it be a park, the beach, a forest, a temple or church, a college campus, or anyplace where there is a calming energy—creates a stillness where I can just "be."

More recovery and strength came as the years went on. And I found many places to soothe and quiet my mind. On horribly anxious days, stuck in rituals, I would force myself to go to the ocean. The ocean had a far greater healing power than I ever imagined. An hours' drive to Half Moon Bay for a 20-minute walk at 11 o'clock at night took the edge off. And I would do anything safe just to calm down the anxiety.

I came to learn that I was taking the edge off and allowing the feel of the ocean to calm the turmoil inside. When I was there, I opened to the sensations that helped me center and feel quiet. I found that letting go of trying to control the anxiety and letting in the peace of the ocean and the quiet of the night were profound healing practices.

Moving In

With a lot of help, I finally moved into my new apartment. My mother had stocked it with plenty of towels, plenty of soap, and everything in the right place—just as I had visualized it. There I sat, not knowing what to do next. Not knowing how to *be* in an apartment again.

In my experience over the years, I have found that one aspect of OCD, which is not talked about, is that many people challenged by OCD lose their idea of how to *be* in this world. I certainly did. Was I supposed to suddenly be like I was before the onset of OCD? Was I supposed to think that I could cook as fast as I did before the onset of OCD? Was I supposed to function alone in the apartment and be fine with all the routine chores of daily life? How was I supposed to be now, after losing so much trust in my own thoughts and abilities? It became a challenge of one risk at a time to find out how to function again, how to live.

As Phil was my primary psychiatrist and Ron my cognitive behavioral therapist, both men, as well as other friends, continued to support my daily challenges of getting through bathroom rituals, shopping, and one of the toughest risks I faced: taking out the garbage. It is important to note that neither Phil nor Ron enabled me by doing these things for me but rather supported me in my risk taking. They did all the supporting, oftentimes re-educating me about reality. And I did all the sweating.

All of those years of risking in that apartment were intense ERP years for me, as they helped to create new belief pathways in my brain, which, in turn, began to repair the damaged ones. Struggle was hour by hour, minute my minute—not at all uncommon for those who take on ERP. I was not unique.

I had now been functioning long enough to try cooking a meal for a friend. I had been going out to what I perceived as "safe restaurants" as well as eating at home, able to handle making a lot of cheese sandwiches in a toaster oven. A toasted English muffin with cheese, crackers, and I think I opened a can of olives—I called that dinner. Can you believe it? I lived on that for months.

But I wanted to continue to move toward the higher good. If I could cook a full meal like I used to, or even close to the way I used to cook, the higher good would be more than accomplished. It would be a feeling of coming home to what I intuitively knew I could do but what the OCD part of my brain still doubted.

I did a little self pep-talk: "Jim, if you succeed, or at least take the risk of cooking a full meal for yourself and a friend, you can give the finger to OCD one more time!"

So, off to the store I went. With shopping cart and list in hand, I walked the aisles. At first, it felt empowering, even freeing. I was shopping by myself like the old days: chicken, vegetables, potatoes, salad. I loaded my cart with much more than I really needed. My cart was full, and I felt such a sense of empowerment. Then *WHAM*, like a bolt of lightning, I felt panic. I was in the middle of a grocery store aisle with a full cart of food, having a full-blown panic attack! I just froze. I hadn't felt that level of intense anxiety in weeks.

"Oh, god," I thought. "Not now. This is too much. This has caught me off guard. And I have no time to use my tools. I'm scared!"

I did the only thing I thought I could do: I left the cart in the middle of the aisle and walked out of the store, working my way home, frustrated and in tears. What now? How was I going to start again? The day had begun so hopefully, so encouragingly. And now I was soaked with sweat from both anxiety and panic.

I sat in the wingback chair in my living room where I had found comfort so many times. And slowly, but surely, I calmed down. The panic and anxiety diminished. But, like before, I was left with fear. Would it return if I went back to the store? I talked to Phil about my experience. And he gave me an exposure assignment that was very different than going to a store crowded with people and buying a shopping cart full of groceries.

The Park and the Truth

The exposure assignment was intended to show me that the world doesn't operate the way the OCD believes. I think it also prepared me to revisit and, once again, take on the risk of the cooking/shopping exposure. For me, any successful exposure would help.

"Jim, I want you to go to your favorite park and find a bench where you can sit and watch children playing on a jungle gym."

"Just watch?" I asked.

"Yep. Just be an observer. You will see how the world works."

So, off to a neighborhood park I went. It was hard enough to check out the benches and find a clean spot to sit—that was a risk in itself—but I had trust in Phil, even though I wasn't sure what he was getting at with this exposure exercise. I sat there, looking at the children; there must have been a dozen of them. There were wood chips surrounding the play area. Kids of all ages, sizes, and shapes were playing and having a good time. At the same time, I noticed what seemed to be their mothers and fathers, about 20 feet away, tending to other family members while eating sandwiches, talking, and also having a good time. Kids would go back and forth, wanting food or attention from their parents. Some parents would give their kids a sandwich. And their child would go back to playing.

I couldn't help but think, "Are they *crazy*? There is so much dirt and germs out there. And you are giving them food?"

To make matters worse, some of the children would run over to their mother, ask for something to eat, drop it on the grass, then pick it up and eat it!

My mind went off the wall. "Are these parents trying to *kill* their kids? What is this?"

Other children would be rolling playfully in the dirt or wood chips, and then share their food. The parents would wipe their child's hands clean, seemingly without paying careful attention and with no urgency or fear on their faces.

My OCD thoughts turned to, "This ain't right!" I was certain that those kids would be sick in less than a week.

Phil had instructed me to go back to the same bench after a week's time to try and catch the same scenario. I did—and those same kids were out there doing the same thing! No one had died. No one was sick. Everyone was having the same fun as the week before.

What was the lesson? I learned once again that the world doesn't operate in the frightening way that OCD conjures up. It brought back how I used to be and what I hadn't been fearful of in the past. In the '50s and early '60s, I also played on jungle gyms and most likely shared food with my friends. I remembered all of that. Although it frightened me to watch this behavior in the park, I realized that this is how people have always behaved, have always lived their lives, and will continue to live their lives.

Phil's point was, "If you want to recapture how to *be* after OCD robs you of trust, observe children for a while. They will teach you what's true again."

After a period of time—including CBT/ERP with Ron who, together with Phil, was committed to helping me—I got back on the horse and attempted the cooking risk again, this time with smaller steps. I went back to the grocery store and watched how people behaved. Much like an actor doing research for a part, I watched human behavior. How did they respond to each other? How did they touch the products? If something was dropped, did they panic or just pick it up? This time, I took it one step at a time. And I left that grocery store with a bag of food and with only what I truly needed. I walked out of the store without anxiety or panic.

The lessons that came were challenging but simple: Be humble, watch others to learn how to be again, take things in smaller steps, and always get back up and try again.

My Chicken Treatment

The night of cooking approached. I had all the wisdom from my mother on how to cook chicken, potatoes, and vegetables in one shot by baking them together. My memory was coming back on how to do this. I had all the pep talks and cognitive therapy from Phil and Ron that I felt was needed. I was ready to tackle this for the higher good. And I was damn determined this time.

I must tell you that I never thought I could laugh at myself regarding OCD. It was far too serious and painful. In living with this disorder, however, I have gained tremendous respect for anyone dealing with even the smallest challenge. I know the depth of pain. But I have learned from my own experience that there is laughter to be had. And it is a powerful healing force. I have come to understand that not taking myself too seriously, even when living with a devastating chronic disorder, is an essential part of the healing process. To this day, I know I must find a way to find some humor, even in my most challenging times. I must laugh, or at least smile; otherwise, the OCD wins.

With that said, I'll tell you how I prepared my dinner and succeeded. The prep was the hardest: touching the food, especially washing it. How much was *too* much? Believe me,

I was still living in a "too much" stage. I must have washed that poor chicken for 90 minutes. If it hadn't already been dead, I would have scrubbed it to death.

If this chicken had lips, surely it would have said, "Will you just put me in the oven? Bake me, already!"

I was not as anxious as I was tired of holding that chicken under the running water. Something in my mind finally said, "Enough!"

I moved to the potatoes and vegetables. Thankfully, those didn't take quite as long, as I was wiped out from drowning the chicken. Even though I was exhausted, however, I felt a sense of momentum growing. I wrapped all the vegetables, potatoes, and that poor chicken in foil, popped it in the oven. And ... *ta da*. I did it!

I had to smile to myself for the accomplishment of the risk and the humor in relating it to my background. Being Jewish, the word "chicken" was many times used in a funny way and represented a healing, staple food of our culture and religion. Why? I have no idea. However, in my life and in my family, boiled chicken represented something comforting, something culturally Jewish. So, in an abstract way, it took a chicken to help me heal.

The chicken didn't fare so well.

I baked the food at 350 degrees F for about 45-50 minutes. My friend arrived. And we ate by candlelight—on paper plates! I hadn't yet taken on washing dishes. That didn't matter to her or to me. It was the risking, the exposure, the observing others' behavior at the park and the store, the higher good, the accomplishment, and, ultimately, the feeling of a sense of *being me* again.

It felt good.

I did go back to the store with plans to cook again. But word traveled fast. I found many of the chickens in the poultry section hiding under the turkey breasts. Not taking myself too seriously and finding some small humor in the pain have been incredibly healing and life affirming, and something I work on in a respectful way, every day. In this cooking experience, I had to start over many times: going to the store; experiencing the panic attack and starting again with a different risking assignment to gain momentum; learning the power of observation; starting and restarting— all that anxiety, pain, and sweat, all for the higher good.

I know from my experience that the main way to heal from OCD is to change what we believe. In my early years, I didn't yet have the tools and skills to help me shift my belief system. But I was about to get one that I continue to use to this day.

"You Can Start Your Day Anytime"

This was a big one. These simple words offered some of the most powerful wisdom that I had ever heard. And yet they didn't come from a psychiatrist, spiritual teacher, or guru. These words, which created calmness and soothing for my anxiety, came from a stranger whom I had never formally met.

I was sitting in a 12-step meeting and saw an older woman in the corner, knitting. This woman had come every Wednesday night for at least four years. She would sit in the back of the room, never speaking, just listening and knitting. I swear it was as if she was knitting a house. She looked a little like Aunt Bee from Mayberry. Every week, she sat in the same chair in the same place, knitting away.

That night, I was talking about how horrible my day had been. I was filled with anxiety, rituals, and obsessions. And was exhausted from it all. I was feeling depressed, frustrated, and damn angry. Suddenly, Aunt Bee put up her hand for the first time ever. She was chosen to speak.

I, of course, being in judgmental mode, asked myself, "What on earth could Aunt Bee have to say that would make any difference in my life?"

By then, she was knitting the second floor of her house! What came out of Aunt Bee's mouth was one of the most profound things I had ever heard.

She quietly said, "You know, you can start your day anytime you want." Then she quietly went back to her knitting.

My energy, and the energy in the room, seemed to go still for a few moments. All was quiet. Then my thoughts began to judge her statement, just as I had been judging her silence for months and months.

I thought, "How can you start your day anytime you want?" I didn't understand. "If I have an anxious day from 8:00 am until 11:00 pm, and I go to bed at midnight, between 11 pm and midnight, I should start my day then?"

"Yes" was the answer.

That's exactly what Aunt Bee was talking about: "You can start your day anytime you want, even if there is only an hour left, and build on that."

Aunt Bee wasn't Aunt Bee anymore. She was my guru!

To make the conscious choice that I could restart my day at any time was empowering. Start your day anytime you want to. What a concept! But how was I going to accomplish that? Well, one process that was not easy but that clearly worked was to consciously shift my attitude into gratitude. An attitude of gratitude was always a shift away from anxiety. I had to keep it simple. What was I grateful for? I was grateful that I ate. I was grateful that I had a therapist. I was grateful that I had at least one friend whom I could call. I was grateful that I had an apartment. You get the idea. All of that and more refocused my attitude into gratitude.

I could restart my day anytime with a creative thought or action. I knew that creativity was healing for me. But, in my various states of anxiety, it was hard to find the energy to write a movie, direct a play, or make someone laugh. So, what did I do? I used my imagination, which helped me refocus and redirect my mind away from anxiety into creativity. *That* I would choose over anxiety any day.

Aunt Bee, now my new guru of wisdom, had given me a simple yet empowering tool that I continue to use and trust these decades later.

Trust that: You can relearn how to "be" in life, even with OCD. You are stronger than you think. You can take one step at a time, even baby steps, toward starting your day anytime you want.

CHAPTER 7

Ask and Honor

*You get treated in life the way
you teach people to treat you.*

~ Dr. Wayne Dyer

Living in my one-bedroom apartment, I was now doing my best to reclaim my life, which was sometimes an hour-by-hour process. Anxiety and panic attacks would come and go at will. I had no employment as my part-time college teaching job had disappeared. I found myself on unemployment benefits, searching for part-time work at any school. I didn't know if I could endure being in front of a class again. But Phil and Ron encouraged me to continue to take risks, including finding a job.

Finally, and seemingly synchronistically, a job at the university from where I graduated appeared. I interviewed with every last acting technique I could remember and manage as I was overwhelmed with anxiety and fear. I knew that I needed a job, and it was right in front of me. The higher good was at hand. And I was damned if I would allow OCD to get in the way. The determination and intention worked, and I got the job: two classes for one semester. My first class was in television production, which I could easily teach. The second class was in radio production, in which I had no formal training; I had to fake it.

On the first day of class, I was late—not uncommon for those of us dealing with OCD. It was very difficult to break the rituals that kept me stuck in my apartment. I was often up to 30 minutes late for class because of a pattern that I believe is a big part of OCD for millions of people, including myself. It happened like this:

- I started out wanting to be on time. And that put added stress on me, even though my intentions were good.

- I did my best to get ready. But, because of the stress to be *perfectly on time,* my anxiety increased and therefore the OCD fears increased.

- I desperately didn't want to be embarrassed by my lateness, as I felt I would be shamed or judged—two of my biggest fears.

- Simply thinking about the judgment and/or shame that I thought would be coming my way for being late started the disastrous obsession of losing my job. And the stress and the fears escalated.

- I was stuck with high anxiety, obsessions, compulsions, and rituals. And the clock was ticking away. I finally pushed through it all, raced to my job, and, you guessed it, I was late!

How do I explain all of this to someone who doesn't understand OCD? In that one semester of part-time teaching, I didn't explain why I was late. I just covered it up with humor or excuses. It didn't work very well.

Telling the Truth

I have learned a lesson that has served in every aspect of my life. It's called "telling the truth." It took a while. But I came to a place and attitude of, "I don't care if they understand or not. I'm not going to lie, or cover up, or be funny about being late. I'm also not going to apologize for a disorder that I didn't ask for and that I'm working so hard to manage."

How liberating it was to surrender and simply tell students and staff, "Hey, ever heard of OCD?"

How strange and incredible when I made that statement and learned how many people had heard of OCD, or had OCD themselves and were going though the same thing! The understanding came not from everyone but from the majority.

My father, who was one of the most compassionate and sensitive men I ever knew, instilled in me at a very early age that the vast majority of people in this world are good—and good at heart. However, not everyone has the capacity to understand, so it is important to seek out extended family and like-minded people who can.

After that semester of teaching at the university, I was lucky to find an opening at the community college at which I had been teaching before my hospitalization. There is nothing like a job to give you a sense of purpose. I taught at that college for 37 years, worked hard not to be late, and, when appropriate, I was truthfully open about my challenges with OCD. Invariably, I found students coming to me as their OCD and anxiety support person both for help and for hope.

Relationships and Answering the Unanswerable Question

So, let's talk a little more about the word "understanding" and how there is so much expectation surrounding it. The nature of true understanding really hit me when I finally took the risk to try a relationship again. After my hospitalization, I was in no condition to have a woman in my life.

I asked myself, "Who would want to be with someone who still had all these obsessions and rituals?"

In recovery and by reclaiming some sense of independence, I found myself in a new relationship. She was kind and as understanding as one could hope for when dealing with this little-known disorder. With the accumulation of time, therapy, and trust, I was healthy and strong enough to risk having a sexual life again. However, understanding the disorder was a challenge for my partner. The unanswerable question of "Why can't you just stop?" became the issue. It was a reasonable question for her to ask but an unanswerable question for me. I had asked myself that same question many times since the onset of OCD.

The expectation that a loved one is willing or even capable of understanding OCD is also an issue. In my experience with my first relationship after I got out of the hospital, I found that I was still fearful of my symptoms. And so was she. It was difficult for me to go though the checking, and the washing, and other compulsions; at the same time, it was difficult for her to see me do all that stuff. It was clear that:

- As she watched me stand at the kitchen sink and wash my hands, she could not help me to stop.
- Expecting faster recovery at any given time would not work.
- Expecting her to always reassure me was not the answer.

These issues were not unique in my relationship. This was not an issue of blame but more of an awareness and acceptance that one's partner may not have the capacity to understand OCD. It was not an easy task.

So, what was the answer to this inability or unwillingness to understand? I didn't believe that I could make her understand. I knew I couldn't make someone understand everything about something they had never experienced, particularly a mental illness. What method or tool could I use to help this mess?

Later, I learned about things called "boundaries" and "limits." I had never heard of or applied this concept before. I define a "boundary" as "how far you will let someone else go" and a "limit" as "how far you will let yourself go."

I summed up these definitions in the following recipe: "I have no control over how others think, act, or behave, or their willingness to understand OCD. However, I do have control over how I think and how I want to be treated." One easy way is to teach your loved one to _ask_ before they _assume and honor_ your response. Then, you do the same in return.

What a concept! It's called "ask and honor." To exemplify where my "ask and honor" concept came from, let me share the story of a profound experience that changed my life forever.

In 1994, I lost my brother Dale to cancer. He was only 46 years old. Being five years younger, I always looked up to him for his great accomplishments and humor. He was a child psychologist, a wonderful father to his two children, and a compassionate, intelligent, and funny man with a dry wit.

He was my brother. I miss him daily.

Dale's cancer was terminal, and he was hanging on one day at a time. The OCD I was dealing with at the time made me extremely anxious about getting on a plane and flying from California to Seattle to visit him. I call this "the harming fear." Some define it as a "hyper-responsibility obsession." In my case, it was obsessive, magical thinking that I could harm my brother by my presence, or a simple touch, thinking that I possessed some kind of deadly, magical germs. This obsession overwhelmed me. And it restricted me from doing many things with my family.

This was a defining moment. My brother was dying. What could I do? I was filled with guilt and self-judgment about whether I could visit him. It would mean taking the risk of getting on a plane, flying to Seattle, and pushing through my debilitating "harming obsession" that was now in full gear.

I wept for not taking the risk to get on a plane. The shame was intolerable. I did something that I was not raised to do as a child. At night, I got on my knees and prayed to God to help my brother. It was beyond painful for all of us in the family. And my anxiety and panic went through the roof because I was about to lose my brother. I was riddled with guilt and didn't know if I should or could push through my fears to see him.

Then, I had an idea that would last a lifetime. I thought, "Okay. I have OCD. My brother is in bad shape. I should go there and be with him and his wife. But I haven't asked him if he wants me to come."

The key word was "ask." So I did. I called him on the phone.

"Dale, do you want me to come out to Seattle to see you?"

He responded quietly and compassionately, "No, I really don't have a need to see you."

Dale was not trying to take care of me because we didn't have that kind of relationship. I didn't take his response as an insult, for we had a phone relationship for many years. He was simply being honest. I heard it as, "I'm in bad shape and don't want company right now, so let's continue our phone relationship. I'm good with that."

And that's what we did, with our last conversation ending with a mutual "I love you."

Not long after those last words, my beeper went off one night. It was my mother's number. I knew why she was calling. Dale had passed.

My brother's memory lives on. His spirit lives on. His energy lives on. I know at a deeper level that our last words to each other, "I love you," will live on too.

The lesson of asking what my brother wanted and needed, and honoring the answer, was yet another tool for my own recovery and a lesson for all of my relationships.

How does that relate to OCD? Those of us dealing with OCD have to open our mouths and *ask* for what we need and want in order to take care of ourselves. It's empowering. It helps us and may very well help those with whom we are dealing or relating.

We need to say words like these:

- "This is not a hand-shaking day for me. I'm asking you to respect that."
- "I am very anxious right now. Are you willing to help me calm down?"
- "Would you be willing to be my ERP coach?"

- "I need a safe, trusting person who will help me take more risks around my fears. Will you help me?"
- "I don't want you to enable me. But, right now, I need a bit more help. Will you help me?"
- "I have OCD. Please respect that, right now, I'm in pain."

You already know all the asking that you need to do. It's a matter of trusting that you will not fall apart if you don't get the answer you want. Don't be surprised if the answer many times is "no." That's called "good boundaries," and you must honor those boundaries.

I found that the healing was in the asking. Ask first, and then respect the answer. If it's not the answer you expected or needed, let go and find the support elsewhere. On the days where it was nowhere to be found, I would ask God for help. Believe me, in the many alone times I have had through the years, where it was just me and the fear, the only asking was between me and God. That higher power was there to help if I was willing to take the risk. I asked, I meditated, or just calmed my breathing. Then, the anxiety subsided a bit and the answers came intuitively:

- "Take a walk."
- "Get out of the house."
- "Do nothing. It's okay."
- "This will pass as all fears do."
- "You've been here before and know how to handle this."
- "Get to a 12-step meeting."

- "Call someone for a little soothing, or just listen to their problems. Helping them will help yourself."

Finally, a last bit of wisdom from my brother before I close this crucial chapter. Before my final conversation with Dale was over, he offered some words and a compliment that I will cherish for the rest of my life. He couldn't talk for any length of time, as the cancer had greatly weakened him. But two profound ideas came from the brother I admired and loved for 41 years. We said that we loved each other. And then an equally amazing and life-changing statement came from his heart: What he liked most in me is that *I honored the feelings of others*. I still cry over that beautiful compliment, that singular gift. I breathed it in as my lifelong mantra and goal: "Honor the feelings of others as you would honor your own."

Honor the Feelings of Others

In my experience, those family members and friends who have asked, listened, and acknowledged my feelings with compassion are the ones whom I trusted most. Even when I was trapped in the throes of OCD, they did their best to hear and honor my feelings. Friends and family whom I trusted most were those who saw *me*, past the OCD. In other words, in some way they understood that *I was not the OCD*. Just as with other diseases or disorders, one is not the diabetes, one is not the cancer, one is not the heart disease, one is not the depression. We are far more than our illnesses. In my case, *I am me, not OCD*. When I could sense that understanding in others, I felt that I could trust them. And the people in my life who didn't fight *me* but helped me fight the OCD became trusting allies.

My family and friends could provide a compassionate ear that showed me they cared about my feelings; in return, I had to offer that same respect to them. What I learned in so many years of being challenged with OCD is that, if I want help from family or friends, I have to open my mouth and ask for it and not expect an automatic "yes." If you ask for help, and they are not in a place or mood to help you, it is your job to accept that and do your best to seek help elsewhere. For me, it was going to a 12-step meeting, or calling a friend, or going to an online support group, or simply going for a walk. Sometimes people are available for you, sometimes they are partially available for you, and sometimes they are not available at all. When this happens, you need to use your own tools to help yourself. Gently teach people how to treat you. And always, just as importantly, honor their feelings too.

Trust that: We so often assume, presume, think, suppose, and guess what's going on with the feelings of others, when all we really need to do is *ask, honor,* and *trust.* Remember my dear brother's inspired mantra: "Honor the feelings of others as you would honor your own."

CHAPTER 8

The Dark Days: Finding the Light in the Darkness

It is better to light a candle than curse the darkness.

~ Eleanor Roosevelt

My intention for writing this book is to tell my story in a way that might offer tools of hope to others challenged by OCD and information for their loved ones. I want to share some practical, common-sense, and spiritual tools that I have picked up over my years of ongoing recovery. I would be remiss to not include this chapter. I have no intention, though, of boring you with a litany of my hundreds of dark experiences with OCD obsessions and compulsions. The following three scenarios should give you a good idea of what those years were like.

As the years passed, one OCD fear or another challenged me. As you know, these included phobic contamination fears, checking and counting rituals, obsessive thought patterns about harming family members, obsessive fears about religious beliefs, and just plain old getting stuck in the shower for hours on end, ruminating on thoughts that I didn't wash my body correctly or enough.

This way of life went on for many years as I struggled to, as Susan Jeffers says in the title of her book, *Feel the Fear ... and Do It Anyway*. Eventually, I did make major shifts and progress in all of those areas. But some continue to challenge me to this day. And, as I have mentioned, the patient is the last one to see the progress. I am constantly reminding myself, or am reminded by my therapist, that I am better than I was last year, last month, last week, and, many times, the last hour.

I have learned to ask someone whom I trust, "How am I doing?" or "How do I look to you?" or "Do I look as bad as I feel?"

These questions may sound silly to many. But when I hear from a trusted friend, or my wife, that I am looking better or making progress, it can mean the world to me. If I hear that I look depressed, I do my best not to get even *more* depressed or defensive but rather take action and get out additional tools to help in my choice to feel better. That's it. Plain and simple. I just want to feel good—or a little better than I did a day ago, an hour ago, a minute ago.

I'll take it. Each moment counts.

Light Made the Shift

When you are scared at night, alone in the dark, do yourself a favor and turn on a light. Light always made the shift for me. It sounds too simple, doesn't it? When I was struggling the most with deep, dark anxiety, which would often lead to an even darker sense of panic as I was lying in my bed in a dark room, the best I could do for myself was to bring light to that darkness by literally turning on a lamp, sometimes all night, until the morning sunlight brought a more hopeful brightness to my worries.

Being a movie buff, at an early age I remember a great scene from a classic 1963 John Sturges film, *The Great Escape* (a perfect title for all of us challenged with OCD). Based on a true story of a German Nazi prison camp, it told how British, American, and other soldiers bravely and painfully dug several ingenious tunnels to escape. Richard Attenborough, Steve McQueen, Charles Bronson, James Coburn, James Garner, and a host of other great actors brought this story to life. After years of viewing the film many times, the claustrophobic scene in one of the tunnels had the greatest influence.

Charles Bronson played an Italian prisoner who was an expert at digging tunnels from his experience of being imprisoned in other camps. In this particular escape scene, well over a hundred men were riding one by one on a small wagon though the tunnel. With candles lit, it was a long way down the tunnel to freedom. Bronson played "the strong man" to whom everyone turned. And he led the others in digging their way out of imprisonment. What the other prisoners did not know was that he was phobic of the dark. Darkness triggered his panic.

Then it was his turn to ride the wagon down the tunnel. Halfway down, an air-raid siren sounded. All action stopped. The escape was at a standstill until the air raid was over, which also meant that the candles needed to go out. Bronson was left in the dark. This strong, powerful man fell into a panic. He began to weep. But a friend on the wagon behind pulled himself over other prisoners and held Bronson in an attempt to comfort him. A sound could not be made as the Nazis might possibly hear them and halt the entire escape. The air-raid siren stopped. And his friend quickly lit a nearby candle. Bronson grabbed the light, held it inches away from his face, and stared into it, as if he were looking at the face of a savior. He was shaking, drenched in sweat, breathing hard. And, as he stared at the light, he saw hope and slowly calmed down.

It was the light that calmed him down.

That scene would be a metaphor for my own life, about how bringing light to any of my dark times would make what I call "the shift." There were years and years of dark days, when turning on a light, or finding *any* light, felt nearly impossible. At times, I felt certain that there was no light to be found, so I had to wait until the light found me. And, in one way or another, it always did. Whether or not I was aware of it, it found me.

The intention of this section is to look toward the possible. When I challenged OCD, I could start to see some light. As difficult as it was, as hard as it was, as sometimes *terrifying* as it was, I still had to cut through the darkness and move toward the light, to get better. In that spirit, I am going to share three experiences in my early years after hospitalization. They were so devastating and so dark that I thought there was no light to be found. But I was surprised to find strength I did not know I had.

Checking on Highway 9

I was working part time at the college, teaching night courses. The OCD was manageable. But I was only two years out of the hospital. And it was a daily struggle to be on my own and continue my re-entry into life and the living. The college was nestled in the hills of Saratoga, California—a small, charming town and a beautiful campus. To get there, I would drive an easy three miles down an expressway called Highway 9. It was one of the more beautiful drives in my area—a two-lane road that cut through rolling hills, with lush trees and breathtaking mountain views, and a speed limit of approximately 45-50 mph, depending on the area of the road. I had driven this lovely stretch hundreds of times before the onset of OCD.

One night, a new fear appeared. I was driving home when suddenly I felt a light bump in the road; not a jarring bump but a light bump. I drove on for a block. And then a horrific thought came into my mind: "What if I hit an animal?"

I tried to let go of the thought. But, as the old saying goes, "Try not to think of a pink elephant." (Try it with the neurological imbalance of OCD!)

I stopped the car at the first turnaround and went back to check. My first mistake. I drove down the road, looking for anything I might have struck. There were shadows that might have been something. But I wasn't sure. I turned around once again and retraced my path. Those old shadows disappeared and new ones surfaced, which could have been a shadow of a dead animal. My anxiety went from a 3 to a 7, and then escalated to a 9—not quite a 10 yet on the scale of a full-blown panic attack. I turned the car back again, put on my bright lights, and slowed down. There wasn't much traffic as it was now 11:00 pm. I saw nothing and everything. Shadows, garbage, everything looked like it could be a dead animal.

My belief was, "Its death was my fault."

Then guilt crept into the scenario. It started to rain. I checked the same path over and over, 30 times or more. Turning the car back, stopping, backing up, stopping again, turning around, stopping, retracing and looking for anything yet finding nothing. I could not stop. My obsession that I hit something was now in high-anxiety mode. I was at a 9.5. Not quite out of control but damn close.

My thoughts raced:

- "If I go home, the animal I hit may still be alive. Maybe I could save it."
- "I may have just killed a living thing. I have to know if I actually ran over something."
- "Should I check again?"
- "I can't stop."

I was on that road for four hours, checking the same path over and over again. My anxiety was now at a 10. I stopped the car, got out, and started to walk around the area on foot. Rain was now pounding down. But all I could focus on was finding a dead animal that didn't exist.

A police car pulled over next to me. What was I supposed to say?

I thought, "I have OCD. And I'm looking for an animal I may or may not have run over."

The officer got out of his car and asked, "What's the matter?"

"I'm okay. I thought I lost something in this area."

"You can't park here, you know."

"Yeah ... uh ... I ... I know. I'll get going. Sorry."

Now, I was in a full-blown panic. I got in my car and drove on. The officer drove past me. I turned around and drove the three miles—the entire length of the road—to start looking all over again. I was determined to find something to relieve the panic. But I also had a sinking feeling that, if I *did* find something, I would fall apart even more. A double bind.

In the pouring rain, I drove slowly in the middle of the road and came across the body of a dead squirrel or raccoon. This, however, was not the area where I felt the original bump. I pulled over, parked, and got out of my car. From the sidelines, I stood in the rain and just stared at the animal.

My mind raced: "I couldn't have hit this animal. I was a couple of miles away. But what if I am wrong and I *did* hit this animal?"

That's OCD at work. The sound of the rain and wind fell silent in my head as I focused on the body of the animal. I was looking for any movement.

Suddenly, a massive truck passed in front of me and ran over the animal!

I literally screamed, "Oh, God!"

I quickly got in my car and raced to my apartment. I was drenched with rain and sweat. I was in shock and in panic. I was shaking and not knowing what to do with all these feelings. I was overwhelmed with out-of-control emotions: obsessions, embarrassment, guilt, anxiety, panic, frustration, and self-criticism. Finding any light in that darkness was a challenge that I was not prepared for.

"There must be someone whom I can call. Did I run over something or not? I can't take this! Who can I call? Who *should* I call? Who would believe this?"

I called my parents.

My father gently calmed me down and said, "Call Animal Control for the roads."

For some reason, those words—"Call Animal Control"— shifted my anxiety. I started to calm down. I began to come back. The OCD trauma and drama slowed down. The darkness was slowly beginning to dissipate. And things were shifting into perspective.

Why?

In those early recovery years, I did not have the emotional muscle or understanding of the disorder to mentally shift into rational thinking by myself. I had to "borrow someone else's brain." Let me say that again: *I had to temporarily borrow someone else's brain because mine was locked by fear.*

I understand this now, many years later. By calling another person and letting them in on my embarrassing secret, my fear lessened. And I was able to calm down. In this case, the person I called was a parent—my dad. And, at that moment, I was not so alone. I wasn't trapped and alone with the irrational OCD fears any longer. I had voiced my fear. I didn't have to hide and live the dark secret or obsession by myself. With one phone call, my father understood to the best of his ability and didn't judge or enable; rather, he empowered me to call Animal Control myself, and they would take over. I didn't have to solve this on my own. The truth was that I couldn't trust my own judgment. Back on that dark and rain-slicked stretch of Highway 9, I could have told the officer the truth. But, in the crippling throes of the obsession, I didn't have the ability.

I always smile when I hear others casually toss out the words, "You need to take responsibility."

Responsibility = responding—with—ability.

I'm all for responsibility. But that night I was stuck in the trauma of OCD obsessions and compulsions about running over an animal. And I was in no shape to respond with any levelheaded, practical ability. I needed a champion. I needed a little help. I needed to voice my fears. The help wasn't always available for me. But fortunately, on that night, after hours of being stuck in OCD fears, the light came from a phone call to my parents, followed by the Highway Animal Control. And it was over—just like that. It was not a magical beam of moonlight accompanied by melodic violins, coming through the clouds to save me, as so often happens in the movies. But that night it sure felt like it. Finding the light in the darkness surprisingly comes in many forms.

From that horrible experience, an invaluable lesson was forming that I would come to embrace much later. Champions and support networks are vital when I am unable to lift myself up and out of the dark. As I mentioned, they were not always there for me. I had to seek them out. For that, I would take responsibility. The true champion, the true strength, however, was always within me. I would come to learn that much later in my healing.

The Bathroom Flood

Be warned that this next experience is graphic.

Mary was a student of mine. She was also an intensive care unit (ICU) nurse at the same hospital where I found myself some three years earlier. She took an acting class from me, and I directed her in plays. Being close in age, we hit it off as friends. And, although she was not a psychiatric nurse at TC-1 where I had been a patient, she knew of OCD.

After I was released from the hospital, she would check in on me late at night by phone. I was always up late, and she worked late, so it was a good match for support.

I strongly believe that the secrecy of OCD is a major part of the problem, and boy did I have secrets. How could I not? Most of the rituals were so embarrassing, and the obsessions so wild, that I found myself not wanting to admit them to anyone other than Phil or Ron, my two therapists. This was the slow learning curve through which I had to navigate in order to find that the "suppression of expression" is what keeps you stuck. I don't suggest wearing your fears on your sleeve. But the old slogan, "You are as sick as your secrets," is true. Finding a trusted person to whom you can tell your secrets is the challenge. In those dark days, Mary was my trusted person.

Getting to bed was hard for me because the rituals kept me up. It wasn't about actually getting into bed, although that did have its own set of checking rituals. I checked the bed for anything I perceived as dirt or germs, and checked my body for anything I perceived to look different or unwashed or dirty. My trouble with getting to bed was about avoidance of all those rituals. I would stay up very late in order to avoid my bathroom rituals, which included sitting on the toilet for sometimes hours at a time, straining violently to void everything in me, cleaning myself with several rolls of toilet paper. Then, the washing-of-hands game could take additional hours as well.

One night, these rituals became so frustrating, so time-consuming, and downright maddening, that I burst out in anger, "*Goddamn* it!"

In a rage at OCD, I slammed my fist against the bathroom door. I broke the door (not my hand). But the rituals went on. Day after day, night after night, the rituals and fears continued. The more I fought, the more I lost. It was late. I had plugged up the toilet with toilet paper, and the worst possible scenario happened: It overflowed onto the floor. Anxious and panic-stricken, I was now surrounded with my own urine and excrement. It was a nightmare!

Surprisingly, with sweat dripping down my face and body, my pupils dilated, and I somehow snapped into another gear. I was still anxious. But something happened in a flash. Maybe I was just tired of being tired. I kicked into "survival mode." And, amazingly, I started to clean it up. I was disgusted, angry, and anxious. But I was still cleaning it up. I didn't know it at the time, but this was my first initiation into learning that I am stronger than I think.

I called the landlord on site to bring up a toilet snake to repair my clogged toilet. Once that was taken care of, I washed for a few hours (hey, it was better than nine hours of washing at the hospital!) and then, exhausted, called Mary at the ICU.

She had always said, "Call me anytime, Jim. I'm usually just on watch anyway. And if I'm busy I'll get back to you. I promise."

With shaking hands, I pushed the numbers on the keypad of the phone.

Mary's voice answered, "ICU Mary."

"Mary, you won't believe what just happened."

"Slow down your breathing and tell me."

"The damn toilet flooded and ..."

"Oh, God. Your *toilet* flooded? What did you do?"

"What *could* I do. I had to clean up my shit."

"Are you okay?"

At that point, out of pure exhaustion, I began to cry. My tears also came from the comforting and caring words of a trusted friend: "Are you okay?" The inflection of caring in her voice, the connection that someone was there—not to judge but to comfort—and the fact that someone knew of my struggles and I was not completely alone turned that horrible darkness into light.

Mary was the light. A nonjudgmental, nonshaming human soul, who was hearing my pain, was the light. The caring words "Are you okay?" were everything to me. When a trusted person cares and listens, the light is always there.

The Desk

Another example of a dark day brought into light is about guilt and ghosts. Now, hold on! I'm not talking about ghosts as in a horror film. I'm talking about those haunting memories that we so desperately want to let go of and are usually marked with guilt.

In the early days of my illness, I was so afraid of germs that I actually threw out money. Yes, money! Fortunately, only small amounts, such as change or dollar bills that I thought were contaminated. I would see red stains on the bills and obsess that it was blood; my therapist Ron told me that it was common in the printing process to see red dye on some of the bills. Thankfully, throwing out money came to an end.

One of my ghosts had to do with a desk. In high school, Dale had made me a desk from a door and crafted two filing cabinets to support it. For years, I held onto that desk into which, during my sex-addictive years, I hid porno magazines and movies. The OCD mind can randomly pick from your life experiences and give power and guilt to anything it chooses. You see, it gives meaning to meaningless things. That desk was its choice.

After the OCD hit, my hospitalization, and the beginning of my recovery, I was finally in an apartment. And there was that desk—sitting smack dab in my room. I was in the early stages of "finding myself" again, and that desk held a huge weight of guilt and self-loathing from the past. It was a symbol of my shame about my sex-addictive behavior. The cabinet drawer, which housed all of my porno magazines from the past, was now empty. But I would never open the drawer. *Never.* I never touched that cabinet. In my mind, it represented contamination, guilt, and a past that I wanted nothing to do with. But it was there in my room everyday: a ghost from my past.

Then came the "satori," a Zen Buddhist term for enlightenment. The word literally means "understanding." Satori translates into a flash of sudden awareness or an instant awakening. My satori was not exactly instant but close enough. Ron, my CBT therapist, suggested an odd but wonderful thing. We were discussing guilt, the past, letting go, and my desk.

"Hey, Jim. Why don't you throw out your desk tonight?"

I looked at Ron in silence for a moment, which was rare for me. "What?"

"Throw out your desk."

"Ron, are you telling me to take a six-foot-long desk, drag it down my apartment stairs to the dumpster, and heave it in?"

Ron smiled. "Yeah."

"Why would I do that?"

"That desk has many ghosts from your past. What are you keeping it for? Is it some kind of expensive executive desk? It's a door with two cabinets that your brother made about 20 years ago, and it's driving you nuts. Throw it out."

"But this doesn't make sense to me. You can't throw things out like that."

"Yes, you can."

"I *can*. But ..."

"Jim, we don't hold onto things that keep us stuck in the past, and especially stuck in guilt. If you don't need it, and it doesn't serve you, get rid of it. Tonight."

"*Tonight?*"

"Why not?"

So, I went home and, that night, dragged the desk in pieces down to the dumpster and flung it over the side. It was an extraordinary feeling of release, a feeling of letting go of the past, a feeling of lightness and of moving forward. It was wonderful! I didn't have a desk for a while. But I had gained something far more precious: another level of peace and recovery.

The *Tao Te Ching*, written some 2,500 years ago by Lao Tzu, taught me that "less is more and more is less." I don't need things in my life that have an emotional charge to them. I can let go of, give away, or donate those things if they don't serve me. That's the "less is more" part. In turn, I get more in my life the less "things" I have. The relief of letting go of that desk was just the beginning of learning to release emotional baggage.

Through the decades, there have been many dark moments, lasting from minutes to hours to days. There have been compulsions and obsessions that ran the gamut of OCD behaviors. Some contamination phobias brought me to the point of taking out a can of disinfectant and spraying furniture that I thought was full of germs. There have been checking rituals of doors, locks, stoves, cars, and my steps—looking for everything, and anything, and nothing at all. I've had horrific thoughts of harming loved ones, which brought on full-blown panic for even thinking the thought. The list went on.

I empathize at a deep level with anyone who is going through the throes of OCD challenges. And I have yet to hear anything that has knocked me off my seat, as I have either experienced it myself or simply understand the pain in ways that only people who have been there can.

One at a time, my compulsions and obsessions would calm down when I used tools that offered a glimmer of light. Sometimes the best I could do was to be with the fear, and feel the feelings, until eventually some lightness would come. Sometimes it was a compassionate voice of a friend on the phone. Sometimes it was simply turning on a light. Sometimes it was reminding myself to slow down my breathing. Sometimes all I could do was pray. It was an ongoing process.

I learned that nobody changes unless they have to. I had to change. I had to take my recovery seriously or I would be left in the dark. Now, my dark days are more like shades of gray. The light is always available. But sometimes we have to work to find it.

What Does OCD Feel Like?

I once tried to explain OCD to a man who was painting the interior of my condo. José was from Chile, and he took an interest in my disability. He wanted to know what it was like to have OCD. What did it feel like?

For all of you who are challenged with OCD, you know that question is nearly impossible to answer. He'd have to walk in my shoes for about an hour or maybe a minute. However, I tried my best to explain because he seemed truly interested. Standing together in my condo kitchen so many years ago, our dialogue went something like this:

"Jim, what does OCD feel like?"

"Have you ever been really fearful of something?"

"What do you mean?"

"Well, what really scares you? Maybe snakes, spiders, rats? You know what I mean?"

"Oh," he cringed, and his expression turned to fear. "Snakes!"

"Don't worry, José. I don't have a snake in my back pocket."

"So, what *about* snakes?"

"Well, you asked me how OCD feels to me. The only way I can give you a sense of what the feeling is like is for you to imagine something you are afraid of. Are you game? I don't want to scare you."

"No, I want to know."

"Well, imagine I'm holding a bucket of snakes. How would you feel?"

"I would be afraid and probably leave right now."

"Well, I don't have a bucket of snakes as this is all hypothetical in your thinking, right?"

"Hypo ... what?"

"Not real. You kind of doubt it that I have a bucket of snakes behind my back, right?"

"Oh, right! I get it. But I want to know what OCD feels like. Why do you get so scared?"

"Okay." I pantomimed having a bucket in front of me. "I have a bucket of snakes here." I could see José's body tense up in apprehension. "And right now, you look scared, even though there is no bucket of snakes."

"I *am* kind of scared, Jim. I don't know what you are going to do with those snakes."

"If I said I'm going to throw this bucket at you, how would you feel?"

José's eyes widened. I could almost see the adrenalin soaring through his body.

"Oh, no, no, no ... don't do that! I may have a heart attack or die or run. And I won't paint your house."

Remember, I had no bucket, no snakes—only words and an image that created a chain of fear in José's mind and adrenalin shooting through his body.

Smiling, I said, "José, I'm not going to throw the bucket of snakes at you."

José breathed a sign of relief. "Oh, *thank* you, Jim!"

"José, the anxiety you are feeling right now is just the tip of the iceberg. OCD plays with my imagination. It used to be for hours and hours, all day long. That feeling you just had in your imagination is an example of the feeling people have with OCD. It's pretty complex biology. And it can be about any thing or any thought."

José was silent for a few moments, and then said, "But, Jim, you look just ..."

"Fine. I know. I don't look afraid. But, believe me, there are many, *many* times I feel like I'm dying inside, scared to death of something that isn't real or true."

"I know that feeling, Jim."

"Well, José, we have more in common than we thought. Don't we?"

"Yes. But no snakes in this house, right?"

"No snakes, José. All is well."

"Are you well, Jim?"

"I'm getting help, José, and working hard to get more prizes."

"Prizes? What kind of prize do you get, Jim?"

I was quiet for a moment, and then said, "Well, José, I get better."

Trust that: The dark days, hours, and seconds can and will pass. I have come to find that not one of my fears or phobias since 1982 has ever come true. Not one. *Ever.* Trust that there is always light that comes from the darkness, even if you can't see it in the moment. It will appear if you allow it in.

CHAPTER 9

"You're Late!"
The Power of Honesty

*Honesty and transparency
make you vulnerable. Be honest
and transparent anyway.*

~ Mother Teresa

"You're late!"

How many times have I heard those words coming from frustrated family members, friends, students, or coworkers through the years? How many times have I said it to myself with a charge of guilt attached to it?

After I was released from the hospital, it was time to find a job again. Unemployment benefits were the game for a while until a part-time job opened at the place where I graduated—San Jose State University. I was hired to teach two classes.

It was the first day of class. I had a full television production class, and the stress was way up somewhere in the stratosphere. Anyone who knows OCD knows this: More stress creates more anxiety, which triggers the OCD button to obsess and do compulsions or rituals to control the anxiety. In my case, it was washing my hands.

Class started at 9 am. But the stress started the week before, and especially the night before. The rituals started at 7 am: Get in the car, race 30 minutes from my apartment to the university, park the car, run to the Television-Radio-Film Department, take a breath, and look like I was the "calm, cool, collected teacher."

After washing some very raw hands, I managed to throw a monkey wrench into the rituals for the higher good, forcing myself to turn off the water. This time, the higher good was my job! By then, I had less than 30 minutes to get to school. I rushed out of the house, trying my best not to get into a "checking ritual." I raced down the freeway with one eye on the speedometer and the other eye on the road, hoping not to be stopped by the police.

Finally, I arrived at the university and pulled into the parking lot. I literally ran across campus, which I knew so well from my years as a student, and went into the double doors of the Television-Radio-Film Department building. The class met in the TV studio. It was now a little past 9:00 am. But I was starting to breath easier because I knew they would be waiting. Why wouldn't they? It was the first day of class! I took a breath to transform into "the cool teacher" and entered the room.

The room was empty!

I rushed to another room. Empty again!

Now, the anxiety that I thought I left at home was back. It was my first job after hospitalization, and I was too late for my class. I went into an office that I shared with a fellow teacher, with whom I had taken a class years earlier, and he consoled me.

I asked, "Where did they go?"

He calmly answered, "Oh, it's no big deal. It's the first day. Students are impatient. They'll be back next time. Don't worry."

Well, that made me feel like crap and a little better at the same time. I knew how much I had to work on being on time. It was one of the first wake-up calls. There was work to be done.

The students did come back. But I was still holding onto a secret that I didn't want to share with them: "lateness."

I found that the issue of being late was, in large part, because of my sleep cycle. In the early days, after the sleeping and eating structure that TC-1 enforced, I reverted back to what I now understand many people with OCD have trouble doing: maintaining a "normal" sleep cycle that works with most work schedules.

I was staying up very late—way past midnight—doing rituals, and then recovering from the anxiety of all those compulsions even later, only to start more rituals and compulsions to get to sleep. Then, morning would arrive, accompanied by the anxiety of having to get to school, and more rituals would start. It was a vicious cycle.

I would eventually break through and get to class. But, when I got home, I would sleep in the afternoon for hours, trying to make up the time that I lost the night before. After all these years, I now know the adrenalin that feeds anxiety is lower at night, so I wanted to extend that relief by staying up. Also, I stayed up to avoid rituals. The longer I stayed up, the more anxiety was produced. It's a balancing act that I continue to work on to this day.

In those early days of getting back to work, the stress could trigger what I call "the spin cycle": stress = anxiety = obsessions/compulsions = more anxiety = being late = more stress. Some days, I was up to an hour late for class. I have no idea how my students hung in there with me. How was I to explain all of this without getting a shitload of judgment back in my face?

Should I have said, "I tried to get to work on time. But I spent two hours checking the stove to see if it was really off, when I logically *knew* it was off. But I didn't really *trust* that it was off." Or, "I know I'm late. Why wouldn't I know I'm late? I was washing my hands for three hours this morning because I was trying to control the anxiety that comes with OCD."

So, what was the answer? How should I have explained? Was having OCD just an excuse for being late? Or would anyone understand that it was a real mental illness and disability?

These days, when I go anywhere, I'm either on time, or 10 to 15 minutes late because I continue to do CBT/ERP. I've made progress. It all depends on the stress and how I choose to handle "the spin cycle." Today, I have more tools to work with.

The Courage to Be Honest

The solution to the problem of holding onto my "secret disability" and not sharing it with others is summed up by one word: "honesty." I am now retired from teaching. But, during my several decades as a college teacher, I told all my students that I have OCD. *I used honesty.*

"I have a mental illness called OCD. I work on the recovery process daily. I ask for your compassion and understanding. If you, like me, have any anxiety problems, I am here for you. If you want to learn more about OCD, you can ask me after class."

And they did! I was shocked how many students also had OCD, thought they had OCD, had family members with OCD, and/or had challenges with anxiety! My honesty about my OCD opened the door for them to see me as an ally or a teacher to trust and to whom they could talk about their issues. When appropriate, I would try to lead them to professional help. I was shocked at how many students, teachers, and staff had OCD and anxiety disorders and were afraid to be honest about them until they heard me share my story.

So, I continue my CBT/ERP around lateness because the "higher good" is about reclaiming my power. The lessons I have learned over these many years can be summed up this way: Being honest and truthful with others and myself about the disorder are major leaps forward in recovery and freedom.

I have rushed, pushed, and sweated with anxiety and guilt to be on time rather than being honest about having OCD and my limitations.

Recovery from this disability is about "progress not perfection." It's about taking one step at a time and working on the willingness to "risk." It takes an openness to try different approaches and modalities. If one approach doesn't work, be willing to try something else. For me, it all started with relearning how to be honest.

Remember: "You are only as sick as your secrets."

Trust that: The power of honesty will, in many ways, set you free.

CHAPTER 10

12 Steps to *The Touching Tree* Movie

*When the student is ready,
the teacher will appear.*

~ Buddhist proverb

I was now learning to live with a side order of OCD rather than a full plate.

However, as Phil, my psychiatrist, told me many times, "Jim, you have learned to function and live with OCD. But there will still be some fears. Always remember that there's no way over fear ... only through it. Someday, you'd better stop calling it "risk taking" because you will run out of life before you run out of taking risks."

"Challenges" is a better word. But, honestly, I still use the word "risk."

In Chapter 5, I mentioned attending 12-step meetings and shared how I met people who would open me to a new way of thinking. I want to tell you a bit more about the program as it truly changed my life and how I looked at the disorder. And, perhaps more importantly, it led me back to my passion of movie making.

In this chapter, I am not in any way promoting or advertising 12-step programs. Believe me, they are not for everyone. As I have mentioned, I was encouraged to start with the 12-step program Al-Anon.

"Al-Anon?" I asked Phil. "Why the hell would I go to Al-Anon? I don't have anyone in my family who drinks. I have OCD. I don't get it!"

As usual, Phil gently smiled and reassured me that it was a good place to start the 12 steps. In Al-Anon, they talk about relationships. And I had serious relationships with fear, with anxiety, with OCD.

Phil's suggestion: "You can take a look at the first step that reads, 'I am powerless over the alcoholic. And my life has become unmanageable.' Well, just take out the word 'alcoholic' and put in 'anxiety' (or 'fear' or 'OCD'), so it would read, 'I am powerless over anxiety. And my life has become unmanageable.' You can do *that*, can't you?"

I thought for a moment and accepted that he had a good point. But I was still hesitant and had a million questions. "But the OCD is becoming more manageable."

"Sure it is. And that's a good thing. But, in that moment of fear when you are anxious, doesn't it feel *un*manageable? That's what we are talking about."

So, off I went to my first 12-step meeting.

After four years of Al-Anon, I moved on to Co-Dependents Anonymous (CoDA). In those days, there was no Obsessive Compulsive Anonymous (OCA) in my area. And CoDA seemed like the logical choice as that 12-step program focused on relationships, letting go of control, letting go of fixing others, lovability issues, setting boundaries, setting limits, and awareness topics such as "progress not perfection." Sound familiar?

To me, it was the recipe for my personality with or without OCD, especially the "progress not perfection" and "letting go of control" parts of the program. I've been part of CoDA since 1992. And I'll continue for the rest of my life. It's simply another tool in my healing box.

Some call 12-step programs "a simple program for complex people." You sit in a room with people you generally don't know. But, in a strange way, you *do* know them. It's in their eyes, words, and stories. Familiarity. You hear your own story through them. And suddenly you're not alone anymore.

"Not alone anymore" ... what a wonderful place to be.

You then get up the courage—or, in my family, the Yiddish word would be *chutzpah*—to tell your story, no matter how embarrassing or humiliating or how unique you feel. And what happens when you tell your story or anxiety of the day? No one blinks an eye. Instead, they accept you without judgment or criticism. They relate to you and with you, even if they know nothing about OCD. What they do know about is fear, the common denominator. Fear and anxiety are universal.

Did ya get that? *No judgment. No criticism.* The others in the group just listened. I was overwhelmed with the comforting thought that I was surrounded by nonjudgmental, emotional support ... and it was free! At first, this shocked me. Where were all the comments, the criticism, the advice? I wasn't asking for it. And it was not part of the program. People just listened.

The power of simply listening to another human being in pain, without judgment or unsolicited advice, was the healing. It was the love. They call it "unconditional love."

The Power of Listening

Sometimes we just need a caring ear. We are not always seeking advice or soliciting comments. Listening can be one of the most powerful and greatest gifts you can offer someone in pain.

I would tell the group about my fears and how I was utilizing a step or steps to help combat those fears. Many times, I would just tell them about a specific fear or anxiety.

Often, as the words came out of my mouth, they would take a right, then a left, then go directly back into my ears.

I was telling others what I needed to hear and learn for myself.

I started to chair the meetings, talking about my fears and how I planned to take them on. Again, I was voicing out loud what I needed to hear and learn for myself. I would talk about my anxiety and fear of flying and how I planned to meditate once I got on the plane, teaching myself what I needed to learn.

The magic of the process was clear to me. Speaking my truth to a group of nonjudgmental people, who were just like me in more ways than I could have ever imagined, gave power to my words. And, in turn, it empowered me to take positive action for the higher good.

What did the other people in the room do while all this magic was going on, as I was learning from my own words? They were validating me.

They validated me by listening.

There was yet another extremely strong component to the program: "connection." The first connection accompanied the term "higher power." At first, I struggled with this concept as it sounded religious in nature. But, with time, I found that the higher power could be anything I wanted it to be and had nothing at all to do with religion. Some people called their higher power "God." Some called it "the universe," "the ocean," or "the 12-step group" itself. It didn't matter what I called it. Anything that was bigger than me, but also part of me, would work.

I started to use the group as my higher power. The collective consciousness of that 12-step group certainly was bigger than I was. So that was my higher power for a long time. But I had so much trouble believing in anything. Finally, I asked one of the 12-step members whom I trusted if we could talk after the meeting.

"So, what's the deal with this 'God' thing? Do I have to believe in God?"

"No."

"But it says 'higher power' in the steps."

"It's not so important what you believe in, rather that you believe in something bigger than yourself."

"But I believe there's a higher power in me too."

"Okay, then believe that. That's a good thing to believe."

Then it hit me. Phil had told me long ago, "Jim, it's all about believing."

Eventually, I came to believe that my higher power was some form of a creating source that I called "God." I believed that God was both outside and inside of me at the same time.

Higher Self

To this day, I believe in a source that I choose to call "God"—a god that is not judgmental, only loving and creating. I'm as much a part of that universal source as every thing and every one. I have come to understand and experience a quiet part of me that is connected to that nonjudgmental, creating higher power. I call it my "higher self."

Let me be clear about this "higher self" stuff. It knows that I am stronger than I think. Got that? *It knows that I am stronger than I think.* Even if I didn't believe it in times of high anxiety and panic, it was still there. I'm not sure if anyone could locate this thing I call "higher self," but it's there inside me all the time.

OCD likes to bully me about this higher-self thing. It kind of sounds like this:

OCD says, "You're not strong enough to handle the wrath of anxiety I am going to dump on you."

My first reaction is, "You're right. I *can't* handle it. The panic and anxiety are just too much. It's terrifying, it's scary. And it feels uncontrollable."

Now, OCD starts to say, "You're damn right you're not in control. I'm in con ..."

But then I butt in before OCD can finish the word "control" because I have an ounce of knowing that what I am hearing is bullshit. "You're *not* in control of anything," I say to OCD. "You're in the fear business. There is a higher strength in me, a higher power in me. And when I calm down, I can connect with it. So, don't give me this 'you're in control' crap! My higher self is in control when I trust it. And today I choose to trust it."

12-Step Connection

I found a connection with my higher power and higher self. But I desperately needed a connection with people. OCD is a disorder where you are so alone with your thoughts and fears that it can be overwhelming at best, crippling at worst, and virtually unexplainable to those who are not afflicted by it. All of this adds up to a sense of being "other," removed or isolated from family, friends, and peers. Living by myself only exacerbated the aloneness. And I soon found myself attending 12-step meetings three times per week.

There was a special kind of connection in 12-step meetings. It was different than simply hanging out with members; it was a deeper connection of "knowing," a sense of familiarity that I felt when I walked through the door.

Many times I would have one of those awful, anxious OCD days and have to drag myself to a meeting, feeling alone and isolated. I'd walk in the door, usually late. Then, from across the room, I'd see people giving me what I call the "12-step hello": a smile and, at the same time, a friendly nod of the head, which was a silent greeting of "Hey, Jim." That little nod and smile made my day. It *shifted* my mood. It filled me up for that moment. It told me that I was not alone. It was powerful and, to this day, invaluable.

There was another interesting aspect to these meetings. At my "home meeting," after someone spoke about anything that was going on in their life, the rest of the group would applaud.

Yes, *applaud.*

I believe strongly that the "suppression of expression" is what really damages the spirit. I always tried to talk at the meetings, even if I said, "Hi, my name is Jim. And I'm having a crappy day."

Then I'd get applause—just part of the tradition! I'm not sure where else you can get applause that easily, especially for a crappy day! In that seemingly small way, it validated my feelings; it made them okay.

Later in my recovery, I became part of a support team, the Campus Assistance Program (CAP) at the college where I worked. CAP supported students who were going through addiction and emotional problems. Most of the students I worked with had anxiety issues. I knew that area all too well from my own experience with anxiety and OCD.

One afternoon, an older student, who was suffering from major anxiety, made an appointment with me. Most of us working on this emotional support committee were simply teachers and counselors who had experience with some form of addiction or emotional issues. We made it very clear that we were only there to listen, comfort, support, and refer the students to appropriate counselors for further help.

Later that afternoon, I met the student at the campus center. I decided to use the most powerful tool that I had learned in therapy and from the 12-step programs: "listening."

She talked to me for four hours, including interruptions to offer "I understand" or "I hear what you are saying." It was getting dark, and I suggested that we continue another day. The woman thanked me as if I had solved all of her problems. Her face had softened from the fearful, anxiety-ridden expression. She couldn't thank me enough for my advice and support.

What advice? I only listened. The advice she needed to hear came from her own words. Her words made those left and right turns, and then went back into her own ears. She heard what she needed to learn and thanked me for advice that I did not give or need to give!

The magic came from me, sitting next to a person in pain, who was asking for nothing more than another human being to listen without judging, blaming, shaming, or criticizing.

Progress Not Perfection

The 12-step program taught me a little slogan called "progress not perfection." And Phil taught me about surrender. When I put these two concepts together, it was a powerful force.

Phil said, "Jim, it's about surrendering, not fighting."

As I mentioned in Chapter 3, I have learned that surrendering is much more powerful than the OCD. Does that mean I just lie down and do nothing? Of course not. It means that *OCD loves a fight and hates surrender.*

So, let me share another inner dialog with OCD. It's important for me to not just angrily rant and rage because OCD will always match my anger. I have to be the adult in the room; I have to be the one who clearly states what I want and what I am going to do. If I would personify OCD, as many do, talking about the disorder as a "he" or "she," I would have a conversation with OCD something like this:

OCD: "Man, am I going to make your life miserable and anxious today!"

Me: "You son of a bitch. I *hate* you! I'll do something to stop you."

OCD: "Like *what*? Wash your hands over and over? You know that won't work."

Me: "I'll use my willpower against you."

OCD: "Right. Like you haven't tried *that* before. It becomes an obsession, doesn't it?"

Me: "I'll fight you until ..."

OCD: "Until *what*? Until you are so drained and so defeated that you can hardly move?"

You get the idea. The idea of surrendering is not about giving up or taking away any of the tools that have helped in my ongoing recovery, such as medication, CBT/ERP, or spiritual and meditation modalities. Not at all. I still have that arsenal of recovery tools.

It is about a different dialogue or belief system that I was aligning myself with. And the conversation changed for the better:

OCD: "Man, am I going to make your life miserable and anxious today!"

Me: "Go ahead. I've been there before. It won't be anything new."

OCD: "*What*?"

Me: "I said, go *ahead*. I know what it feels like. And I can handle it because I have these tools. Been there, done that. I got the tools, man."

OCD: "Like what? Your little hand-washing rituals? You know *that* won't work!"

Me: "Yeah, I know."

OCD: "Huh?"

Me: "I said I *know* it doesn't work as well as just feeling the anxiety and letting it pass. But, if I do it, I guess I'll just have to work on 'progress not perfection.' So I wash my hands. Big deal. I've survived it before. And, with all my tools, I'll slow it down and do less and less and less."

OCD: "What? Progress not ...?"

Me: "Perfection. I know you're not gonna get this. And it doesn't matter if you do or don't. I don't care! All I care about is that *I get it*. I know you hate that word 'progress' because you want control. And you seem to love to screw with me by throwing in fear and anxiety. But I surrender! It's 'progress not perfection.' So, if you are going to bat me around with anxiety, go ahead because I know you'll leave faster if I just feel the feelings and let go. You don't have the power here. I do!"

OCD: (speechless)

Now, all of this took practice, and continues to take practice. But I have found that it was also the basis of CBT/ERP—my main source of recovery to this day. With support, I would expose myself to a fear, feel the anxiety, let it bat me around—or as I call it "surrender to it"— and then, to my amazement, it would eventually pass.

What it took was working with surrendering and remembering "progress not perfection" right out of the 12-step programs I was involved in. Let me say this again: *12-step programs like Al-Anon, CoDA or OCA are not for everyone. But they offered me solid anchors to believe in, which would counter my fears.*

In the beginning, I was afraid and unfairly judgmental of the people in these programs:

- "They are not like me."
- "They clearly will not understand OCD."
- "What do they have in common with me?"

- "What do I possibly have in common with them?"

Phil once told me, "Hang in there. It's never what it appears to be."

Projection Makes Perception

Phil also used to tell me (from *A Course in Miracles* by Foundation for Inner Peace) that "projection makes perception" and asked me to "change the film in the projector in my mind." He knew I came from a filmmaking background and that his example would make sense to me.

I had a projector in my mind with a film running of judgment, negativity, and criticism. So, naturally, with this film playing, how do you think I perceived the people, places, and things in the world? Judgmentally, negatively, and critically.

"Jim, change the film in your projector. Take the negative one off your mind projector, and put one on with compassion, love, and understanding."

I bucked up, swallowed my pride, went to the mental video store, and chose a film called *Give It a Chance*. Now my projector was running *Give It a Chance*. And I was starting to slowly perceive things differently. It certainly didn't come all at once because there was that pesky thing called "my ego." There was resistance. But I did my best to remember "progress not perfection," and I found that my perceptions and presumptions of the world (people, places, and things) started to look different. I felt more open to possibilities.

This "projection-perception" thing was working—if I could continue to keep my ego out of it. I wanted to think of different, positive films to run on my inner projector and stay away from the negative flicks.

To give you an example of how I was running a negative mental film and how "it's never what it appears to be," let me tell you how I was busted—not by the police but by my own cynical projection. I was going to CoDA meetings on a regular basis and teaching at night. At the beginning of one semester, a male student walked into my TV/Film Acting class. He was a character out of a Hells Angel movie, if not the real thing. He looked about nine feet tall, black leather jacket, chains, and an attitude of "teach me or else."

My projector jammed.

I started to perceive a guy who was out to get me, and I was going to be stuck with him for an entire 16 weeks. My perception was that he would slash my tires, and then drag me behind my own car if I didn't teach him acting from this little junior college class. He was damn intimating and scary.

All I could think of as I started my opening greeting to my class was, "Please leave. This isn't the class for you. Take out your aggression on some other teacher, for God's sake. Why me?"

I put on my usual "good to see all my new students" face. You know the look. I was scared inside. And my Monkey Mind was saying, "He's going to take out his *Star Trek* phaser and instantly evaporate me if I don't say the right thing." But my face was saying, "Welcome, students, to the world of acting!"

Talk about acting! In our department we had to accept *all* students, whether or not we were comfortable with them. If you're not familiar with the term "Monkey Mind," it is a Buddhist term that describes a mind filled with screaming, restless monkeys, all clamoring to draw your attention to fear, worry, and everything that could go wrong.

I began all of my classes with a talk about acting and an introduction about me. I offered a bit of spiritual-minded talk that related to taking risks because performing and public speaking are the biggest phobias for most people. During my talk, I glanced over at the Hells Angel guy. And he was not only silent but had a face that reminded me of a disgruntled grizzly bear.

After the first class, new students always had questions. Out of the corner of my eye, I saw the Hells Angel guy in line. I finished with the other students' questions, and the last student left was the nine-foot killer. He towered over my 6'1" body.

I thought, "Is he going to kill me now? I truly don't want to die in a junior college classroom. Or is he just going to stare me down until I have a panic attack?"

I stood my ground as he looked down on me. He spoke in a soft voice that didn't at all fit his image or girth. "So, this is acting for both TV and film?"

"Yep, you get both in one," I said while my adrenalin ramped up for an anxiety attack.

He paused for a second and looked around the studio. "The way you talk sounds like you know Bill W."

At this point, I have to explain for those who are not familiar with the question, "You know Bill W?" Bill Wilson was one of the founders of Alcoholic Anonymous (AA) more than half a century ago. The 12-step programs that came from the original AA model are attributed to Bill Wilson—CoDA, OCA, Al-Anon, or the 50+ other 12-step programs. It's kind of an "inside code" for those of us who are in anonymous programs and want to reach out to others in programs without breaking their anonymity. "Do you know Bill W?" Underneath that phrase is, "I think you are in the program like me."

"Yeah, I know Bill W," I said, with all my fear dissipating.

"I thought so. You sounded like you did."

"Do you know Bill W?"

"Oh, yeah."

"How long?"

"I've been in recovery for three years."

"Fantastic!"

"How long have you ..."

"Well, I've been in CoDA for a lot of years. But you know how it goes. It's ..."

"One day at a time, right?"

"You got *that* right."

"I think I'm going to stay in this class."

"I want you to stay. Hey, we're in the same club anyway, right?"

"Yeah," he smiled.

I found myself hugging this guy, who may have been a Hells Angel. But I didn't care because we connected in recovery. My projection and perception, which was based on nothing more than a judgment based on an image, changed in an instant. In that moment, I saw myself in him. And he saw himself in me.

So, Phil was absolutely right. It truly is "never what it appears to be" and that includes people too.

Service to Others

Participating in 12-step programs was about to guide me to one of the biggest life-changing risks of my life—one that launched me into what I feel is the true medicine of recovery: service to others.

Helping and supporting people with OCD took the focus off of me and made me realize that my uniqueness was not so unique. I was about to dive into an important new chapter of my life: inspiring others to get better from OCD. In the best way I could, I'd support, educate, and help others who were suffering. I believe we teach what we need to learn. And, as I helped others, I was helping myself. It was a pivotal point in my recovery. And I believe it was right on time.

I had heard about the International OCD Foundation (IOCDF), formerly the OC Foundation—one of the world's largest foundations for OCD research, support, and education. Around 1990, I sent the founder of IOCDF some of my films about hearing-impaired children, with the wild idea that I could make a film about a child with OCD.

I never in my wildest imagination thought they would say yes!

The president of the foundation flew to California from the East Coast. And we talked about the cost of producing the film. I was now becoming both committed and fearful of what I had gotten myself into. The foundation advertised an upcoming film about a child with OCD on the cover of their national newsletter; I, on the other hand, was talking to my psychiatrist weekly about whether or not I could really pull this off.

The project would involve writing the script, producing the film with a friend of mine, directing it, and possibly playing a role in the film as well. What was I thinking?

My anxiety about this new project and all it entailed escalated. But I knew that excitement was a big part of my fear and that I needed a good dose of wisdom to stay grounded. I needed a champion, someone not only to tell me I *could* do it but also why I *would* do it when there was high probability for creating additional anxiety for myself.

My idea was to write the story of a child with OCD. I knew that OCD symptoms in children are basically the same as in adults. So, in a way, I was writing my own story. Did I really want to see that on the big screen? Or even on a small screen?

I was at a 12-step CoDA meeting, contemplating all of this—actually, *obsessing* on all of this. I had been attending meetings for years by this time, so I knew some of the faces. In my experiences with 12-step programs, I never really buddied around with the people in the program and yet always felt comfortable with them. They were like-minded people. And it was a safe place. I'd see a face that I hadn't seen in months. And the smile would come from across the room as if to say, "Welcome back, Jim."

One of these anonymous people was Mike (no last names were used in 12-step programs). Mike was an intellectual; I am not. I tried to keep up with his references and philosophies but never really could. Nor did I understand what he was talking about most of the time as we walked around the parking lot of the meeting center. But I liked him. And we connected.

One night after a meeting, Mike and I walked around the parking lot and talked until all the cars had left. The dialogue with Mike went something like this:

"So, I hear you have an opportunity to make a movie?"

"Yeah, Mike. But I'm scared shitless."

"*Shitless*? And the subject matter is OCD?"

"Yes. They want me to write and direct a film about a child who has OCD."

"You have OCD?"

"You know I do."

"But scared *shitless*?"

"Right."

"Tell me, Jim, who else has OCD?"

"What do you mean 'who else'?"

"What are the statistics?"

"I'm not sure. But I think about 2-3% of the population has OCD."

"Do people in other countries have it too?"

"Mike, what are you talking about? It's worldwide. A big deal. It's an equal opportunity illness."

"I know."

"So, what are you ..."

"And you have made films before, right?"

"Yes. But nothing like ..."

"Do you think you can write this script?"

"Well, yeah. But ... I think I can write a script."

"Would a film like this help people?"

"It might. But ..."

"At best, educate them, right?"

"I would hope to offer some awareness."

"People don't know about OCD?"

"There are a lot of people in the closet with this disorder. The public doesn't know a lot about it."

"Okay, Jim. I have all the information I need. Do you want my input?"

"Always."

"The issue is that you are scared shitless but have the opportunity to make a film that will not only help people but educate them as well. You can help people become aware of a mental disorder that is universal and affects people of all ages. Your fear is overpowering you, making you doubt whether you could do this or not. True?"

"Yeah."

"And your recovery is all about facing your fears. True?"

"Yes."

"So?"

"*Hmmm* ... so I guess I'm making a movie!"

"Good. I'll come to the premiere."

It was an anonymous man named Mike who, in a parking lot, set me straight about facing my fears. When we are open to it, wisdom and champions come from unexpected places.

The film was made and went on to win eight national and international awards. A filmmaker never truly knows how a film will be received. I knew, however, after the film was released and I traveled to Minnesota to show it at the Obsessive Compulsive Foundation Conference, that it was important and touched many people.

Before the film was shown, a woman approached me and threw her arms around me, thanking me for the film. She told me that her parents would have never known about her OCD without this film.

That was good enough for me.

Phil Kavanaugh once said, "Helping one person can make an infinite difference."

That day, I felt it from the woman who came up and hugged me.

The film is entitled *The Touching Tree.* And, even though it was released in 1992, it holds up to this day. You can view it for free on YouTube.

Trust that: Projection makes perception. You can choose to change the film that is running in your internal projector. And you'll see people, places, and things in the world in a very different light. Trust that helping one person can make an infinite difference. Helping others helps ourselves. It's a powerful medicine for OCD.

CHAPTER 11

"Me, Being Me, and Letting You See Me"

*I laugh, I love, I hope, I try, I hurt, I
need, I fear, I cry. And I know you do
the same things, too. So we're really
not that different, me and you.*

~ Colin Ray

I was at a conference where Bob Earll, who wrote *I Got Tired of Pretending*, was speaking on intimacy. His message was summed up in eight words: "Me, being me, and letting you see me." What a great definition for opening to intimacy in any relationship, as it promotes honesty, authenticity, and openness.

I found that I could use this message for OCD too. In my experience, I have come to understand that we are "as sick as our secrets." Our relationship with the disorder of OCD is as unique as our relationships with our friends, lovers, partners, coworkers, and all others.

It always amazes me how freely the majority of people can talk about most illnesses. But, when it comes to *mental* illness, if they discuss it at all, they talk in "hushed tones," not wanting to be overheard, as if the very topic is taboo:

"Did you know he was bipolar?"

"She must be depressed. Just look at her."

"Look at what he's doing. He must have that OCD. *Shhhhh.*"

And while it can be much the same with other illnesses—perhaps cancer, certainly AIDS—discussing mental illness tends to make most people far more uncomfortable than talking about other health issues. At times, it seems as though people think they might "catch it" if they say the words too loudly. There is a serious stigma about mental illness in our society, and hushed voices and whispers only perpetuate the ignorance or misunderstanding of disorders that affect millions of us—family, friends, neighbors, and coworkers alike. OCD, like any other health crisis, is an equal opportunity illness.

Over the course of many years, I learned that holding in my fears and phobias was hurting me more than connecting and communicating with others. It wasn't "me, being me, and letting you see me."

I remember a student who wanted to take my TV/Film Acting class at the college where I was employed. It was a popular class. But, as with all acting classes, you had to open your heart to feelings you may have never felt before—not only in front of your peers but in front of a camera as well.

One day, a very shy, 20-something-year-old girl came to the class with her mother. Both she and her mother knew that I was the teacher who had been "open" about my disability and had no qualms about this being public information. In fact, I wanted people to know about my illness so I could help those students in the beginning stages of OCD.

The mother, with her daughter at her side, stopped me in the hallway and spoke to me in a hushed voice. "You are Jim Callner, right?"

"Yep, I'm the one and only."

"I was told that you know about OCD."

"Yes, I have a nonprofit educational foundation that helps people with OCD. I have OCD myself. I've been recovering since 1982. And I have a feeling that I'm not the only one here who has OCD. Is that true?" I said these words as I looked at her daughter.

Shyly, her daughter said, "Well, yes. I have OCD."

The mother chimed in, "Do you think she belongs in this class? Do you think she could handle it?"

I looked at her and her daughter and said, "Listen. Everyone has *something*—from hang-ups to disorders. In performing arts, the main issue is anxiety. It's show business! You happen to be with a teacher who has experienced plenty of anxiety himself and who teaches tools on how to calm it down and work with it. I also have the same disorder your daughter has, so you lucked out. There's nothing your daughter could tell me that would knock me off my chair. I either have it or have worked through it. So, yes, your daughter is in the right place."

I then asked the daughter if I could ask her an OCD question.

She timidly agreed.

"Do you have contamination fears?"

"Yes."

"I bet mostly in the bathroom, right?"

She paused with a surprised look on her face. "How did you know?"

"Because I have the same thing—not as bad as it used to be. But it's still there. How many rolls of toilet paper do you use?"

Her mother was very quiet.

Her daughter's face started to soften. "I don't know. Maybe three on a bad day."

"I've got you beat! When I was really sick with OCD, I used up to four or five rolls!"

The girl seemed shocked. "*Five rolls!* Do you still use that much?"

"Nope."

The girl then asked me the magic question: "Well ... what happened?"

I looked at her directly and smiled. "I got better."

Now the girl was smiling. There was a connection, without shame, without judgment.

She took the class. She got an A.

Maybe my methods are unorthodox; I'd rather call them "compassionate."

"Me, being me, and letting you see me." No need to be afraid. If you surround yourself with those who judge you, you know that those are not the people to be around. Seek out the people who get it, the like-minded individuals who have no need to judge and are willing to let you see them too. On that day, the student saw herself in me. And I saw myself in her. And something called "trust" happened.

Trust that: You are only as sick as your secrets. When you have the courage to practice "Me, being me, and letting you see me," you will be taking the first step toward getting better.

CHAPTER 12

You Do the Best You Can Given the Conditions You Are Under

I trust that everything happens for a reason, even when we're not wise enough to see it.

~ Oprah Winfrey

To date, there have been five defining moments in my life. Relationships and career have been, and continue to be, important to the fabric and stability of my life. But, when I talk about "defining moments," I speak of those pivotal life experiences that shifted my consciousness into another way of looking at life, another way of seeing myself and others in the broader picture.

The onset of OCD and the recovery process, which includes writing this book, are two of those defining moments. The death of my brother in Chapter 7 certainly shifted my perspective on life, including my own mortality. My marriage at age 50 to my wife Jeanine continues to show and teach me about the nature, meaning, and potential of love and intimacy. The last defining moment happened while writing this book. My longtime best friend, confidante, caretaker, and only surviving parent passed away: my mother.

My father died in the mid '90s. His passing was more of a blessing after years of suffering from Parkinson's disease. I will forever miss my father, my teacher. All he gave and taught me, and his unwavering depth of compassion— perhaps his greatest gift—are now instilled in me.

Although sad and a tremendous loss, my father's death did not hit me as hard as the devastating sense of loss of my mother. This chapter is not about the personal details of my mother's peaceful passing. It is more about my reaction in terms of OCD, so that hopefully it will provide help and solace should you be faced with the passing of a loved one. Such a profound loss can greatly exacerbate the symptoms of OCD. And, more than anything, this chapter is meant to reassure you that you are not alone.

As knowledgeable as I thought I was after years of living and coping with OCD and the OCD recovery process, my reaction to my mother's passing took me by surprise. OCD is sneaky and invasive when it comes to something this big, particularly the death of a loved one. One of my friends, a psychologist who specializes in helping people with CBT/ERP and is challenged with OCD himself, calls this kind of setback a "backwash"; that is, you are so overwhelmed with a backwash of emotions that, no matter how much you know or *think* you know about OCD, the flood of emotions and fears, some crippling, can backwash into your life.

I remember sitting with Phil Kavanaugh at his home office and arguing with him about knowledge. My position was that "knowing" was all you needed; his position was that "it wasn't about knowing at all." I now understand what he was saying. In truth, it's all about the *feeling*. During the writing of this book, and as my mother peacefully passed away, the feelings were overwhelming. All the knowing in the world didn't preclude or minimize the staggering feelings of guilt, helplessness, and grief. I had to experience the depth of feeling in order to cope, and, in turn, to better understand.

I had to feel it. It was and is the only way.

The Harming Fear

During this time of backwash, one major OCD fear that I had been struggling with for decades reappeared: hyper-responsibility—or, as I refer to it in my life, "the harming fear."

Ron, my CBT therapist, offered this: In his 40+ years as a therapist, which included helping people with OCD, he had seen many fears. One of the most prevalent was the fear of death, accompanied by what he would also call "the harming fear." I believe—as does my OCD therapist friend Sharon Davies of The OCD Treatment Centre in England—that our biggest fears are being alone, suffering, and death. I clearly have all of those fears.

If you are challenged with OCD, you more than likely have experienced some form of the harming fear; if not, let me try to explain from my own experience. Simply put, the harming fear is a manifestation of OCD in which I have irrational obsessions that I could harm a loved one with my thoughts or actions.

My obsessions always included thoughts and fears of germs and contamination. OCD convinced me that I could harm someone by simply shaking their hand, being in close proximity, or breathing on them. I would fear sitting on someone's sofa, believing that a particle of dust or lint from my clothes would fall onto the sofa, leaving behind potentially dangerous germs. You name it, and I could conjure up some kind of fear of contamination that could harm others. This would morph into a full-blown obsession that I'm at fault, leaving me and them disabled in some way or, in my worst OCD fears, possibly dead. None of this was rational or logical. But there you have it: OCD at work in the most painful way.

Usually this harming fear was with a family member or another loved one. Mine always manifested with my parents or any relative who was very old or very young. The more vulnerable they were, the worse it got.

One of the strange components of this obsessive anxiety and secrecy of emotions was acting as if everything was fine, all the while panicking inside. The energy it took to conceal my anxiety while secretly battling the fears would leave me exhausted.

Although my battle with OCD fears would wax and wane in the years following the onset, there were many times when I struggled with hugging my mother with my hands open. I would manage to hug her. But usually it was an abbreviated hug with my arms around her and my hands closed into a fist so I would not really touch her. It wasn't the kind of hug where you freely and openly hold someone you love. My mind raced with ways of not allowing my hands to touch her, terrified of spreading germs, of harming her. With time and effort, I pushed through the fear of touch. But there was always the heaviness of the harming obsession riding shotgun alongside.

It wasn't about "knowing," as Phil had told me so many years ago, but rather about feeling and risking; exposing myself to a fear, and then practicing that exposure, which gradually, with time, becomes less frightening.

Can you see where I'm going with my story? My mother was at the end of her life. The OCD harming fear was triggered. I understood the trigger and what lay beneath: the fear of death. Wonderful! Two of the most common fears of those living with OCD: the fear of harming and the fear of death. Now what?

In my public talks about OCD, I shared my perceptions and beliefs in life after death and the eternal. But, when the experience became so close, so personal, the extreme sense of loss left me in a state of childlike aloneness and severe sadness. I was 56 years old, my mother passed, and suddenly I was six years old, asking "Where did my mom go?"

Naturally, this isn't specific to OCD. Most of us have some fear or questions about death: "What happens? Where do we go? Is there life after death?" Most of us choose to believe in something that offers comfort in a time of uncertainty. Unfortunately, my OCD obsessive mind didn't make it that simple. And I heaped a massive helping of guilt on top of all the questioning.

I'm still questioning. But, deep down at my core, I do have a belief system. When the backwash of OCD moved in at my most vulnerable time and tried to latch on, I knew how difficult it would be to get back to that belief system, my foundation. When the debilitating fear, anxiety, depression, and grief—the Monkey Mind of disaster—and obsessions of guilt began to settle in, I tried to repeat a simple slogan or mantra, working to bring myself back to the present moment: "Thanks for sharing, OCD. But I'm not buying it."

These simple words seemed to slow down the obsessions, move me back on track to the present, and give me what I needed to do at that moment. I needed to feel the pain. I needed to feel the pain until it dissipated. There was no other way. In being true to myself and the grief of my loss, I had to feel it. I had to acknowledge and respect the *feeling*. No matter how difficult, there was no way around it other than going through it.

"You Give Me Strength"

For over a decade after my father died, my mother continued to live in California. She then decided to move to Oregon to be closer to more family. It was a courageous decision for someone in her 80s.

I kept in touch with her by phone and Skype, and one time I was able to overcome my fear of flying to visit her in Oregon. She flew back to California twice. Although my guilt of not seeing her in person continues to haunt me, our relationship was as strong and loving as ever. We found that our communication, no matter how we did it, was the most important aspect of our relationship. The regularity of the connection was crucial. But, regardless of our regular connections and the bonding that took place with each contact, I still felt the overwhelming sense of guilt that I didn't do enough. I have to let go of that guilt a little each day. It has not been easy.

Then my mother, at almost 90 years of age, was moving toward the end of her life. It was apparent to me and other family members that there were no dementia symptoms but rather the slowing down and wearing out of her heart and body.

It's funny, but I never saw my mother as old. She used to say to me, "Jim, I'm going to be 90!"

I would just take it in stride and ask her how old she felt.

"I feel like I'm 42."

"I guess you should *act* like you're 42, Mom!"

As her health declined, my harming fear was triggered. Jeanine and I talked about a trip to Oregon. But the fears were getting stronger each day. The anxiety was moving into a state of high anxiety bordering on panic. And it was relentless. Should I go? Should I not go? My guilt was over the top. Some family members didn't and couldn't understand. How does one explain the devastating effects of OCD symptoms when their mother is declining in health? The simple answer I found is this: *You can't explain.*

I looked at places to stay in Oregon and tried to imagine myself there. I would drive near my local airport and imagine myself on a plane. I made out a detailed map on Google Earth of how to drive to Oregon, thinking it would be easier. But all attempts seemed to exacerbate the already constant state of high anxiety and increase the terror of the harming fear.

This was my mother and my best friend. And, although I didn't want to accept it, I knew deep down she was moving toward the end of her life. I had to do the right thing. But, at the same time, I was denying the fact of what my 12-step sponsor reminded me: "Jim, you do have OCD. If you *could* go, you *would* go."

I was doing everything but being honest with myself and trusting my intuition. I decided to go to the source and take the approach I did with my brother so many years before. I Skyped my mother and told her, "I don't think I can get out there, Mom." I couldn't come to see her in Oregon. I was apologetic, guilt ridden, and ashamed. But, I had to trust my gut and admit to her: "Mom, it's the harming thing ..."

My mother, forever protective of me, said very firmly, "Do not come here, Jim." She knew the symptoms all too well. She knew how they affected me and how far back it would set me if I visited. During the Skype call, she became adamant, in her way, for me not to come to Oregon. She understood the challenges of OCD. Even though I trusted what she said, the guilt ran through me with fury.

Along with my father, my mother had been there at the onset of OCD. She was the one who patiently stood outside of the bathroom door, handing me a dozen towels, one at a time, to dry off from a single shower. She was the one who had to make the decision to put me in the hospital and let go. Enabling me was not working. Under the care of Phil, the hospital was the right place for me. She and my father had to *trust and let go.*

It was now my turn to *trust and let go.*

How could I have done all of this risk taking and exposure therapy and not get past the hurdle of going to Oregon? Simply, it was more than I could handle.

So, with help, I got honest with myself about what I was capable of doing at that time. I trusted my mother's insistence that I not come to Oregon. I trusted my support therapists, who told me, "Don't bring your anxiety out to your mother." I trusted my wife, who echoed the same sentiment. I trusted my mom's main hospice caregiver, who told me not to bring my anxiety to my mother because it would cause her to be anxious and worry about me. I trusted my 12-step sponsor.

And, the only way I could start to trust myself was to follow the wisdom, "You do the best you can given the conditions you are under." So, that's what I did: the best I could. *at the time*

Every day, for virtually four months, I called my mother either by phone or Skype. My sister gave me a great gift by telling me that I had the ability to make my mother laugh, which would help her. I knew then what my job was: to give my mother lightness, give her a daily laugh, help keep her in the present, and be present with her. I would help her with her anxiety. I would let her know how great she and my father were as parents. We would talk about nothing and everything. And, each day, I would tell her that I loved her. Even during the last few weeks in hospice when she was unresponsive, I would call and tell the wonderful hospice caretakers to tell her that I loved her. The mutual love between my mother and me was clear, genuine, and real.

While I was comforting my mother, as always, she offered up comforting words to me. She told me two wonderful and life-affirming things.

During one Skype call, she said an amazing thing to me: "I think that talking like this, on Skype, is actually more intimate than when we talk in person, Jim."

I agreed.

And, in the last call I had with her, we talked for over 50 minutes. And she said the most loving and important thing I could have heard during that difficult time: "Jim, you are the one who gives me strength." They were beautiful, powerful, and soothing words.

But, even so, I struggled with tremendous guilt and shame for not actually being there with her.

"You do the best you can given the conditions you are under." Now, what does that *really* mean? My mother was under the condition of being close to the end of her life. And I was under the condition, which I never thought would happen, of having a relapse into the devastation of OCD obsessions and compulsions. So, what was the best I could do with that scenario? I had to get honest with myself and trust that I was simply not capable of supporting my mother in the way my fantasies described: going to Oregon in person, making her laugh, holding her hand, and saying, "I love you."

I did the best I could given the conditions I was under.

Then, the challenge was one that I've had so many times before: How do you explain a debilitating OCD symptom to family members who don't understand?

It is difficult at best to explain OCD to anyone. My mother witnessed it, as she and my father were with me at the onset and saw the devastation firsthand. They knew the many faces of OCD, the symptoms, and the toll they took on me. But what about other family members?

My brother Dale was a psychologist. And, although I was hospitalized for nearly six weeks, he never called or saw me. Why? He understood "detachment." I now understand why he didn't get involved in my disorder. He couldn't "fix me." Lovingly, he took himself out of the picture and let people outside of the family—those with the expertise—help me. I know it was the most loving thing he could have done. My sister tried to help. But, other than professionals, the disorder was out of everyone's league, so she did her best to offer comfort to my mother and father.

As with many families, there is a major denial factor as well. I believe that the stigma of mental illness exists as much today as it did back then. I am high functioning in many areas in my life. But I do have times of high stress that trigger anxiety and OCD symptoms. I have to work extraordinarily hard to challenge the anxiety. Like many others, I look and act just fine. I can work, I can drive a car, I can interact with others, I can shop, I can laugh, I can take care of myself. The problem is the turmoil on the inside. If the symptom or symptoms could be seen, then perhaps there might be more compassion from others. However, in my opinion and experience, we have a long way to go with what I call "the unseen disabilities."

In the midst of my grief and guilt about my mother and not being able to see her in person one last time because of the OCD, how could I get my family to let go of their judgment and understand? I was tormented by even more ruminating questions: How could I explain in any logical, reasonable way, that I had no choice but to stay at home while my mother was in the care of hospice? How could I explain not being able to see her in person? How could I explain something I could not explain to myself?

The letter below was a response to one of my cousin Joey's emails. He virtually pleaded with me to come to Oregon to see my mother. It explains "the harming fear" and why I was unable to travel to Oregon. To protect my family, the name and relationship has been changed.

Letter to Cousin Joey

Joey,

I appreciate that it's hard for you to understand why I am not coming to Oregon. I struggled so hard with this in July. And that's when my therapist, who has been with me for half of my life, recognized that I was becoming very symptomatic of the OCD "harming fear," which, in my case, is directed toward our family and especially my parents. This is how it goes, Joey:

The harming fear causes me to obsess about my responsibility for somehow contaminating (with my germs) a vulnerable family member and causing their illness or death. Who more vulnerable than my mother at this time? Is this irrational and illogical? Yes! But OCD is a disorder that prompts my brain to actually believe this in times of severe stress. And, believe me, Joey, it can paralyze me. My mother is very aware and understanding of this fear, as she was there from the onset of my OCD.

My mother and I have replaced an in-person connection with phone and Skype because she clearly knows about my fear and has adamantly told me, in no uncertain terms, to not exacerbate my fears by coming out there. Believe me, I grilled her twice about this in a long Skype conversation. And she clearly told me, "Do not come out here, Jim."

So, we have used Skype and the phone daily since mid April. We have loving and clear communication. And I believe my mother is reassured that I will continue my recovery from OCD.

To understand this a bit more, Joey, let me share an incident that I've never told you about because, at the time, I thought you were too young to understand. It had to do with when my father died. The short version is that I took the risk of putting gas in my car before seeing him for what would be the last time. I was afraid of chemicals, also a common fear with OCD. But that day I took the risk.

I saw him in a rehab hospital, and he couldn't talk and was very sick. He shook my hand, which I now realize was for the last time. Not long after, he died. My disorder kicked in with a vengeance. And I thought I had caused his death because of some gas that might have been left on my hands.

Irrational and untrue, yes. But, to this day, I never put gas in my own car and at times still have to wash my keys. I never get near gasoline. It has become another phobia. That's OCD! Maybe someday I'll be able to get past that with continued help. But it has disabled me for 15 years. I know this is all hard to understand. But I'll tell you the full story someday if it doesn't upset you.

My mother and I have established a long-distance relationship that serves us both well. And she has told me many times of the appreciation and gratitude that she has for you and everyone involved.

I know you may perceive me as the funny relative with problems. But behind that mask is a harsh reality of a serious mental illness that, while much better after 30+ years of very hard work, is not cured by any means.

And what they call "the harming fear" around death is one of the main symptoms of the disorder. I have not completely conquered that one. I try. But I have much more *work to do. I had to put my trust in my two therapists and my psychiatrist. I could not take the chance of going back into a severe OCD state. I wish I was more able at this point in my recovery. But the reality is I'm not. And that's really hard.*

Because my mother was there from the beginning of the OCD, she understands on a deep and profound level. As my psychiatrist said, "The healthier I am, the more reassured my mother will be." This is very important to understand.

I don't want to bring my anxiety to my mother at the end of her life. It would be unfair to both of us. I want to bring her what I've learned about peace and living in the moment. And I seem to be doing that for her.

The substitute for not being able to be there in person is to be as present and available for her at all times, which I will continue to do, and will do until it's time for her to transition.

I talked to my mother Saturday for almost 50 minutes and Sunday for an hour. Her main hospice caregiver was amazed that she could be on the phone for that long. She was weak at first on Saturday's talk. But then we began talking much like we always have, with my attempts to be as present and light with her as I could.

She said something wonderful to me at the end of our conversation that I'm sure she has said to you too: "You are the one who brings me strength. And we'll talk tomorrow."

That's our relationship, Joey, with me always encouraging her to live in the present moment, appreciating everything. She took that as a mantra yesterday. And I'll keep reminding her as long as she's here.

I don't feel that I will have any regrets, as I have had more heart-to-heart talks with my mother in recent times than ever before. Even she said, "When we see each other in person, we never have these heart-to-heart talks. But on Skype we do."

Again, I appreciate and love you dearly and know where you are coming from. I hope you understand a little more now about what I'm dealing with, and that I am doing the best I can given my condition. I would never be angry with you for expressing your feelings. I'm glad you wrote to me.

Love you,

Cousin Jimmy

For a while, my cousin did take in these words. But my expectations that they would last were much too high. Long ago, Phil told me something about family and my disorder: "Loved ones are many times the last people to whom you want to turn with the expectation that they will help or understand." I was shocked. I thought that they would be the *first* people to turn to, the first who would understand. I believe in some cases that this may be true. But I also believe and have experienced that, at times, I had to let go of my expectations of my family, including my mother.

Additionally, in my experience, I have found that families have too much invested. They try to *fix* or *not fix* family members in countless and often inappropriate ways, as the thought of seeing a loved one suffering with a disorder renders them powerless. They simply don't know what to say or do with that emotion. And, in truth, understanding is just too much and far too painful. How could I expect my family members to understand "the harming fear" when I couldn't understand it myself?

I could explain my symptoms of OCD to an audience of 500 people at any given conference. But what was happening in my neurobiology, emotions, and spirit was difficult to understand and explain. My family has done the best they could do. But shame, blame, and judgment have no place for those challenged with OCD. It does not help. It only hurts.

If you have a choice between critically labeling someone or treating them with compassion, always choose compassion. Labeling is stigmatizing. Compassion moves us forward.

The best words I have ever heard on this subject came from philosopher Søren Kierkegaard: "If you label me, you negate me." Simple, but true.

The Bottom Line

After my mother's passing, the OCD harming fears that were triggered—along with a Monkey Mind gone wild with guilt, fantasy, and obsessions—had slowed to a more reality-based pace. It was crucial for me to check into what was "real," as I have always been a person who can easily slip into a fantasy realm, imagining myself in other scenarios. For example, I saw myself at my mother's bedside, comforting her with my humor and presence; I saw myself comforting my family and sister at the memorial. But the reality that I had to accept was that, at this period in my life, I did not have the *capacity* to do those things. I could only do what I could do. And I had to make peace with that. I have found, after so many years with this disorder, that is the reality I must face.

A terrific book by T. Cole-Whittaker is titled *What You Think of Me is None of My Business*—a phrase to live by when it comes to trying to explain OCD symptoms to family and you're not getting the reaction or compassion you want! My expectations of a few family members were unrealistic.

Trying to fully explain this disorder is very difficult, especially to family. Understanding is possible only if the listener relates in some way. I do believe that, in the years I've been speaking to audiences, many do understand. While OCD is neurobiological, there is no doubt that at its root is fear and a need for control. People can relate to the fear and control issues.

Family love and connection are powerful. And I know my mother wanted that for our family. My mother passed away very much the way she intended: peacefully and without pain. I am eternally grateful for that. My sister and I have a renewed relationship and are moving forward with an increasingly deep connection. The disguised family member I talked about is also far more understanding. Sometimes that's all you can ask for. Remember: "progress not perfection."

I am forever grateful to my sister and Oregon family members for all of the love and dedication to my mother. I feel that I did my part. And I do not diminish the work I did and the love I offered to help my mother long distance. I'd like to believe that, collectively, we helped ease her anxiety to pass on in the way she had hoped.

Trust that: You do the best you can given the conditions you are under at any given time, knowing that you will learn and be stronger from them.

CHAPTER 13

OCD Challenged Me to Face My Fears

*You gain strength, courage, and
confidence by every experience in
which you really stop to look fear
in the face. You must do the thing
which you think you cannot do.*

~ Eleanor Roosevelt

Doesn't that sound strange? A disorder teaching you how to face lifelong fears? But that's what OCD has been doing for me ... whether I liked it or not.

I grew up as an anxious and a hypochondriacal child, never really facing the fears that life presented to me. For example, for most children, going to camp was an exciting and a wonderful time; for me, it was a terrifying and lonely experience. All I wanted to do was to get home to my mother—to my safe place. As Phil told me long ago, I was a fearful child who grew up into a fearful adult. Then came the onset of OCD, which exacerbated many of those fears.

In my experience, OCD is a fear-based disorder. But what has become interesting to me over the decades is that I know deep down that my fears, phobias, and obsessions are not based in reality. Yet, I still doubt. I still have a gnawing distrust that spins into larger obsessions or compulsions.

At first, I found OCD horrifying; then, with some recovery, I moved up the "emotional scale" and found it challenging. With more recovery and more practice of recovery, I have accepted that OCD is part of my life—and my recovery, though not a straight line, is progressing. Sometimes I'm in the groove and sometimes I'm not. But I am always working to move forward.

Obviously, I would not wish OCD on anyone. But, for me, it is a medical condition that has forced me to challenge a lifetime of fears. Those of us who are challenged with OCD know how lonely and painful—and I mean *physically* painful—the symptoms can be. We also know how resistant we can be to this process called "recovery." For instance, one day I can let go of my old OCD shower rituals and take my shower time down to what feels like a more "normal length shower." But, the next day while showering, I might get stuck in anxiety and take longer. These OCD waves can come and go, depending on a variety of stress and environmental factors as well as reasons that are just unexplainable.

Before you feel discouraged from reading this, let me tell you what threw a monkey wrench into my cycle of fears and disrupted the OCD cycle. It's considered one of the most effective ways to treat OCD. And I've been using it for decades and will continue to use it for these reasons: *I want to face my fears, I want my life back, and I want to feel good again.* I would encourage anyone to take that last line as a motivating mantra: "I want to feel good." It's that simple. For me, it has helped me to remember my goal.

CBT and ERP have worked the best for me. They work hand in hand. Let's take CBT first, as it was usually the normal progression of how I worked with my therapists Phil and Ron and presently with my coach. I think of CBT treatment as the "thinking" part of recovery. It is very different from traditional talk therapy where you explore your emotional state and family history. It is more about exploring a specific irrational fear that I believe to be true. It involves changing my belief systems. Ron or Phil worked with me to expose the irrational thinking of my fears. In essence, they helped me invalidate the fears, and then move into what we called "risking," which was really the ERP or the "doing part" of my recovery.

I needed someone, a person whom I trusted (Phil and Ron), to yank me out of those entrenched beliefs and fears and back into reality. The encouragement to challenge my fears is what CBT therapy is all about. I cannot tell you how many times I said these words to myself or heard these words from others: "Just stop thinking, Jim."

Well, it's a swell idea. But for me to "not think" is just not possible. In fact, all of us have an estimated 60,000 thoughts a day. For me, however, there was another way to manage my OCD thoughts.

Thought Replacement

Years ago, Ron came up with a better idea (better than "just not thinking") that we called "thought replacement" in our CBT work. Thought replacement is just what it sounds like. I found, or was given, a thought to replace the negative, fearful, and destructive OCD thoughts. When I used thought replacement, it helped me stay connected to "reality" rather than the intrusive OCD fears. Believe me, the one thing that OCD really can't stand is a reality-based thought!

Thought replacement helped me trust truth more than fears. Let me give you an example of how it worked for a friend of mine.

I've been helping a friend with CBT/ERP for some years now, as he's been helping me. For the sake of my friend's anonymity, I'll just call him Frank. Frank is a psychologist and has helped scores of individuals around the country who struggle with OCD. He has lectured about the nature of OCD and has literally stayed in people's homes for weeks at a time doing CBT and ERP therapy. Frank has often helped me with my OCD challenges. But the interesting thing about Frank is that he a psychologist, an expert on OCD, an accomplished speaker on the disorder. *And he has OCD.*

My friend has come to me on many occasions, seeking whatever wisdom or spiritual support I could offer him on his rougher days. One of those rough days had to do with Frank's OCD fear and obsession about cancer and "harming." The following is all based on a true experience.

Frank was working in a hospital and had to walk past the oncology wing every day to get to where he was going. The hospital's wing had a sign that clearly read "Oncology." Frank's fear, the obsession, was the thought that, by simply *looking* at the sign that read "Oncology," his family and his extended family would get cancer. That was the irrational OCD thought that needed replacing. Once Frank was willing to buy into a replacement thought, I encouraged him to start the "doing" part of this treatment, which is ERP, and actually face his fears. In Frank's case, it would be walking past and looking at that sign every day.

Since I have OCD, I have learned never to doubt or make fun of the irrational thoughts of someone else with OCD. The OCD—not Frank—was talking to me about a sign that read "Oncology" and its power to cause cancer in his family.

My process with Frank was the same thought-replacement strategy that Ron used with me. I talked to Frank about reality- and nonreality-based thoughts. I know from my own experience that, if I offered Frank a reality-based thought and he was willing to trust it, it would eventually punch a hole in the OCD. Here's a bit of our conversation:

Jim: "So, Frank, how many people do you think walk past that 'Oncology' sign every day?"

Frank (after pausing): "I don't know ... a hundred. No, wait a minute. Maybe a couple hundred."

Jim: "Really? That's all?"

Frank: "I'm just guessing. Maybe a couple hundred, maybe more. It's a big hospital. And a lot of people have ..." (Frank couldn't even say the word "cancer.")

Jim: "Okay, let's double it. Let's say 400 people walk by the sign every day."

Frank: "Okay. So?"

Jim (in a serious tone): "Have you ever read any newspaper, journal, or magazine, or seen anything on the Internet or television about anybody getting the 'C' word or any other illness from looking at that sign?"

Now, what is vitally important here is that I said this to Frank in all seriousness and due respect, as I have had many obsessions that were just as bizarre or irrational, having felt the frustration and pain caused by these crippling fears.

Frank (after pausing again): "Well ..."

Jim: "I mean, think about it. Four hundred people walk past the sign every day. Have you seen *anything* from a media source about *anyone* getting *any* type of illness from looking at that sign, Frank?"

Frank (starting to laugh): "I see where we are going with this, Jim."

Jim: "May I take that as a 'no'?"

Frank (laughing): "Yeah, that's a 'no.'"

Jim: "That's a reality. If you had that kind of 'superpower' to look at a sign and cause someone to have an illness, we would all be in big trouble, wouldn't we? In fact, if anyone had the power to look at the sign or anything else and cause another person to be ill, it would be all over the Internet, newspapers, television, radio, cell phones, and road signs."

Frank: "So what do I do?"

Jim: "Well, I suggest you do the same thing I have to do: Face your fears but with a new thought. And the new thought is: 'I don't have the power, the sign doesn't have the power, and nobody has the power—except maybe in the movies—to give someone an illness just through their thoughts, or we'd be hearing about it.' That's the new thought."

Frank: "I guess ..."

Jim: "The next step is the action step, the 'doing' part. You know the routine. To really shift that brain chemistry of ours, we have to 'walk our talk.' No more talking or thinking about doing the action but walking through the fear and trusting that you'll always come out clean on the other side. Tomorrow, before you take this on, I encourage you to give me a call for a little pep talk, so I can remind you about thought replacement. You'll then walk through those doors and take a look at that sign. But keep the thought replacement going. And, after you've done the exposure part, feel those feelings, Frank. It's just the energy of anxiety, and all energy passes through you. Feel the feelings, stay with the feelings, and they will pass. I promise. Feel free to give me a call because you'll have a 'win' under your belt. So, you know the drill. But you will have to practice, practice,

practice until the fear doesn't become a fear anymore. I'm on your side, Frank. You know that."

So, my friend had some recommended CBT thought replacements, and the trick was for him to take the next step: the ERP, the "doing" of this process. As I told Frank, he could call me anytime before or after he walked past that sign. But, ultimately, it was up to him to trust and push through the OCD fears.

Why It Works for Me

Why does CBT/ERP work. And why has it worked for me? Well, let's keep this as simple as possible. Here's the thing that I had to trust—and that I encourage you to trust: When you take the risk to change your belief system, and then take the action of facing your fears, sometimes one at a time, it will change your brain chemistry. It's called "neuroplasticity," the new science showing that the brain is malleable (not stagnant or fixed). Simply put, by facing your fears, you can literally change the neuropathways in your brain for the better. And I'll take any form of getting "better" over fear and anxiety!

Clearly, if CBT/ERP worked for me, it can work for you. In fact, it's been the most powerful way I've found to break my OCD patterns.

Here's an example I went through while writing this book. My triggers were pulled from the stress, loss, and grief of my mother's passing. That was the obvious analysis my therapists came to, along with my own thoughts and feelings about the passing of my mom. I never imagined that the symptoms would come back this strong and be so unrelenting. But it happened. I had to get back to some serious recovery work.

I was taking showers, which lasted for an hour and 15 minutes, and truly struggling—washing the shower walls and going over my body with soap again and again, using two bars of soap. Then I stepped out of the shower, feeling frustrated, discouraged, exhausted, and loaded with guilt, shame, and self-judgment. And the long shower was just one of the compulsions. I didn't feel as though I had relapsed back to 1982, as I knew too much about recovery. But the relapse was frustrating and a struggle nonetheless.

My self-esteem was also struggling. I was the one who was supposed to know how to manage OCD! I was "James Callner, the filmmaker of *The Touching Tree, The Risk,* and *In the Shoes of Christopher,* and a lecturer on OCD." I mean, if anyone should know how to deal with this, I should. Right?

"Think again, Jim!" said the inner voice, which had been quiet for years but was now screaming bloody murder in my head.

As Phil had said so many years ago, "It's not about knowing. It's about feeling."

And now I also understand that it's about *trusting.*

I was having daily high-anxiety attacks. And it felt like I had forgotten all of the tools I learned over 28 years. Where the hell did they go? The Monkey Mind was out of control with guilt. I was having disturbing nightly dreams, and then waking up, thinking, and obsessing over suicidal thoughts but not enough to act on any of them. To say it scared me horribly would be an understatement. But deep down I knew and trusted that I could come back. I had done it before with CBT/ERP. Once again, CBT/ERP was the key to my shift. And, believe me, all I wanted was a little shift, a little relief.

I prayed for relief. I talked to God, asking for strength and connection, which I still do nightly.

I prioritized, in my mind, the fears that I could take on. Next, I decided on the most doable or less frightening compulsions or obsessions that I was willing to take on. The key words were "willing" and "doable."

So, I began CBT/ERP with the help of two therapists. Here's how it worked for me: One of my major fears was going to the bathroom and being contaminated. At the time, I had a ritual of using a whole roll of toilet paper to clean myself, and then an unhealthy dose of obsessive thinking that, if I didn't take a shower after I went to the bathroom and wash everything off, I might be contaminated and harm myself and others.

I suggest "doing what is doable" in every moment, knowing that facing your fears is the way out. The easy ones, the less anxiety-producing fears, may be more doable, and that will give you confidence to take the next step to the tougher ones. I found that it was about being honest with myself and what I would be willing to take on, pushing the bar to not get stuck in the "easier mode." The brain will adjust once you practice facing your fear.

Now, on to facing those fears: I can tell you from my experience that there was no way around my fears. I needed to go through them, just as Phil had told me years before.

The good news is that, after each face-off, I came out stronger with a new, deeper knowing and feeling that these fears were just FEAR.

So what does the acronym FEAR mean? I've been saying it to audiences for years: "False Evidence Appearing Real." To me, OCD has always brought me false fears; that is, fears that have no basis in reality. None of my OCD-related fears have *ever* come true. Many examples are in this book. But here are a few more.

For years, I have had a fear of driving past a garbage truck with a fear of germs coming off the truck and into my window and contaminating me. Another false fear I've had for decades is the fear of contaminating someone if I shook his or her hand or vice versa. Now, let's get real about this false obsession of shaking hands. When I see rock stars, movie stars, the president, or even the pope, who shake hundreds if not thousands of hands, it doesn't come to mind that they are going to get sick and perish. What *does* come to mind is that my contamination fear about shaking hands is a complete lie. There's no evidence that it's true! Even so, the fears appear real. So real, in fact, that I'm compelled to obsess over them and do compulsive rituals to calm the obsessions.

Once I challenge the OCD, I weaken it. That's what CBT/ERP does. It weakens OCD every time you do it. Whether you do a full exposure or part of an exposure, you are taking the strength out of the OCD and shifting your brain chemistry for the better. It takes a commitment to daily practice. But it does get easier. The brain habituates to normalized thought and behavior, and the OCD calms down.

Let me repeat this: *It takes daily practice. But it does get easier.* For example, if I drop my keys in a parking lot, an OCD thought of contamination will rush in for a few seconds. That's when I have to get tough with myself and challenge the OCD. So, you know what I do? I pick up my keys off the ground and move on ... and feel the feelings.

Let's face it. Facing your fears alone is extremely difficult. I know that some people have done this. And it is possible. But I found it to be extremely hard. I had to find a coach—a friend or family member—to help me move forward.

After doing CBT/ERP on my own for some time, my wife offered to help as my coach. She was not just a cheerleader, saying, "Good for you, Jim," but she reminded me to stay present, focus, and differentiate between OCD and reality. For example, before I got help with coaching for taking a shower, I would wash every part of my body many times, over and over again, trying to hit all areas. Of course, this was not needed, causing great anguish and pain to my body as well as wasting infinite amounts of water. But OCD doesn't much care about your anguish—or an astronomical water bill. It just relentlessly compelled me to keep washing.

I needed to "borrow someone else's brain," so to speak, to literally re-educate myself on how to take a shower. I first watched how my wife took a shower. Yes, I wanted and needed to see what "normal behavior" was. I needed a mental anchor. Remember, OCD distorts one's thinking.

I watched her splash soap on her body, not obsessing about hitting every body part or every square inch. Next, with clothes on, we rehearsed taking a shower in a different order than I was used to. Jeanine walked me through the steps of this new approach. One thing that challenges OCD the most is changing a previously dysfunctional routine that you've been stuck in. It's a good thing for recovery. We called it "the Top-Down Jim Shower" because I started with washing my hair first rather than last, and so on.

Afterwards, we did some CBT, which I audiotaped so I could listen and review it later. This tape was very important to have because when Jeanine was not available to help me in person, I could review her logical comments on how to take a shower on tape. I recommend this kind of process.

We discussed that the oils on my body don't want to be washed off nor is it needed. Showers are meant to refresh and do a basic cleanup. And our body oils are there for a reason: to protect the skin, not to be scrubbed off. She gave me the thought replacement that "only one glide over any part of my body was enough." It was also unnecessary to hit all the areas because the soap would eventually splash on all areas or the water would move the suds down and off.

Of course, in my OCD state, I asked, "What if the water or soap doesn't get to all the areas?"

Her answer was direct: "It doesn't matter because the oils in your body will protect you, remember? There's nothing that will harm you or others when you're out of the shower." That was the CBT thought-replacement part. And seeing her shower was the belief part that I had to choose to trust.

Then came the "doing part" or ERP—the big trust. I had to trust that my wife, who had been taking showers like this virtually all of her adult life, had never been contaminated or had harmed anyone due to her shorter shower routine. *Ever!* I could trust this intellectually. But, to trust it on a deeper level, I would have to experience it. I had to take the ERP step. I didn't think, at the time, that it was possible to take a 10- to 15-minute shower. So, before I could take the leap of faith to take a shorter shower, I had go back and really look at some beliefs I had learned along the way.

Years ago, Phil and the 12-step programs taught me about "power." Remember: OCD stripped away my power to trust my own thoughts. I believe we all have a higher power that comes out at times when we least expect it. We find ourselves doing and achieving things that we never thought possible.

As my sister would say, "Jim, you can do more than you think you can."

It's true. But trusting it, believing it, and acting on it was not so easy. I needed to do it to break OCD.

The Higher-Power Concept

I have had higher-power experiences several times in my life. My best example was building a house with my wife. Me? Supervising the building of a house? Are you kidding? I have OCD! House building—even if you are watching someone else do it—is, well, dirty! Yet, the *higher good* propelled me to the *higher power* within me. And we now live in that house.

Your higher power can be inside and/or outside of you. As I've mentioned throughout this book, I choose to call that energy "God," but I believe this idea is worth restating. It doesn't matter what you call it—"source," "the universe," "love," "nature," or "energy." It's more important that you choose to believe and trust that there's something there. It's unexplainable. But it's there. I have to emphasize that this is not a religious thing for me. But, if religion is part of your life, I hope you use it for your well-being. For me, all that truly matters is that I feel it, acknowledge it, and do my best to believe it, trust it, and use it to my advantage.

It is my belief and feeling that some sort of higher, benevolent power or spirit—all about good—exists and can be accessed. Yet, with that said and with all the believing, OCD was robbing and distorting my higher power and trust.

Sometimes I just couldn't reach God. I was too anxious, too self-involved, and too scared, so I had to make a person my temporary higher power. Don't be scared; it's okay to do that. In fact, Phil once suggested that I make *him* my temporary higher power. All that meant was that I was in bad shape power-wise and that I had to make the choice to trust his decisions temporarily and act on them. I had to trust him as my temporary higher power. Then, I had to make my wife and coach my temporary higher power and trust that what she said was the truth. I needed to take her direction unconditionally. Again, I had to borrow her brain for a while until I could trust my own brain power.

The Bully

Ever notice that OCD is like a school bully who never grows up? *Never!* It wants what it wants. It's insatiable.

It's like a brat at a candy store, screaming, "I want candy! I want candy! I want candy!" until the parents simply can't take it anymore and buy the kid some candy.

In my case, the bully was screaming, "You need to check! You need to wash! You need to obsess day and night! You will contaminate someone if you just touch them, so you had better do it my way, or I'll give you something to *really* panic about!"

Now, if I choose to respond to that OCD bully with some self-talk—and believe me, I have—it goes something like this: "Wait a minute, jerk! Do it your way, or you'll give me even *more* fears? Something *worse* to worry about? No, no, no, no! I know what you really are. You're just a bully. I don't talk to bullies. I'm bigger, more thoughtful, and more aware. But you don't understand those types of words, so I'm just going to ignore you and replace you with another thought. I know you'll be back. And I'll treat you exactly the same way."

Let me pose these questions as they were posed to me:

- Would you discuss a real estate deal with a bully?
- Would you ask a bully for advice about your taxes?
- Would you consult with a bully about a medical procedure that you are about to have?
- Would you talk with a bully about your relationships?

These absurd examples have helped me put OCD in its rightful place. *OCD is a bully that doesn't tell me what to do.* Why? Because I'm bigger than bullies. And I don't have time for them. Never waste your time arguing with a bully. The bully is relentless. You just can't win. How you *can* win is to put your time into trusting your higher power and what is real, and ignore the bully. It takes work; it's not easy. I get all that. But it's the way to recovery.

CBT/ERP and the Shower

Here I was, in the shower, with Jeanine coaching me from outside of the shower. Not as much fun as you might think, as there was ERP work to be done. Jeanine reminded me that all it took was a single glide of soap over any part of my body. And I didn't have to hit all of the areas. She reminded me that soap was running down my body, washing away any dirt. She reminded me to stay in the now, in the present, and feel the warm water running down my body along with the soap. Again, she reminded me it was the OCD—not me—that was keeping me stuck. She was doing her best to remind me of what I already knew. It was up to me to trust it and act on it.

"Jim, are you willing to interrupt the ritual for the higher good?"

Good question—and in the middle of a shower, no less, when that damn bully was dimming my brain. But I had to trust her, remember? So I kept going, knowing that, after the shower, I might feel some anxiety. But it would pass. In my case, I didn't feel major anxiety after the shower; instead, I felt the exhilaration of winning over OCD. I love those "wins."

Practice, practice, practice is what I always heard from my mentors. What I have experienced with practice is that fear and anxiety gradually dissipate. Essential for

ERP success are willingness to take direction and trust it, willingness to work on mindfulness and staying present, and, most of all, trusting what my coach was telling me was true.

In time, I came to trust the coach within myself and only occasionally needed CBT/ERP reminder sessions with Jeanine. I learned to trust *me* again.

Going for It

I want to tell you about an experiment I tried with much success. You may want to talk it over with your therapist, psychiatrist, or coach. It didn't come easily for me. And it took a lot of trust and willingness to do. But it was effective in challenging my OCD magical thinking with a jolt of reality thinking. This experiment showed me the lie of OCD thoughts. It would confirm that I really *could* trust what my coach Jeanine was saying as the truth. It was, if you will, a visual "trusting of reality."

Here's what happened: I came to the point of being sick and tired of being sick and tired. I know you know what I mean if you have OCD. I decided to do something a little more radical. I call it "going for it." Specialists would call it "full-on exposure." (I like my slogan better.)

I asked Jeanine if she was willing to help once again with the shower ritual. I had cut back somewhat on my exhausting shower routines. But I was still tired, *very* tired of taking 30- to 38-minute showers. My goal was 20 minutes. But I was having a lot of trouble getting there.

I came to the point that I talked about earlier in the book: willingness. I was ready and willing to "go for it"—to trust what Jeanine was telling me for the last eight months in CBT sessions:

- "The oils on your skin protect you from germs."
- "OCD sees things that are not really there. Just keep going."
- "One glide of soap on any part of the body is more than enough."
- "You don't have to cover every part of your body with soap."
- "People take showers in three minutes and get clean."

The list went on. But I was still not really trusting her until I did my experiment. I took a small video camera and set it up for Jeanine to videotape me while I took a shower. Remember: This time, I was *going for it.* I pulled out all the stops with trust and pushed through my fears, with Jeanine taping it all. When I did this experiment, I went from 38 minutes to 23 minutes, the next day 17 minutes, and the following day 14 minutes. What was happening? What was working? Well, I was reviewing the videos in between my showers.

Now, keep in mind that it was also "exposure" for me to look at those videos. I remember trying this some time ago and deleting the video before I could look at it. I simply didn't want to watch myself with the disorder. But, this time, I was in the "going for it" mode. I watched it with a more clinical, detached viewpoint. And, as usual, it was not at all frightening (with the exception of seeing how huge my stomach had become!). The key was that I saw the truth that Jeanine had been telling me for months. The camera in this situation did not lie.

Soap was going down my body. And I saw that I had no need to wash over and over again. When I rinsed my shampooed hair, the water took the soap off in about four to six seconds, not the two to three minutes that I had been rinsing. The washing and rewashing so many times were clearly unnecessary because I was seeing reality in the video. It showed me how OCD was lying to me. It unmasked the disorder, exposing it to the light. And, by watching the video, something shifted in me. I literally had to see it to believe it.

I realize that this technique might not be easy, depending on one's level of struggle with OCD. But I can tell you that, seeing OCD for what it really is, and the truth of the reality, made a huge difference in my recovery. As always, I recommend that you talk with your therapist or coach about this technique before trying it.

Willingness is the first, essential step to ERP. All those mantras and affirmations I used moved me toward action. However, ERP is about *doing*, remember? It's about *taking action*, feeling the feelings of anxiety, and allowing them to pass through you. They always will. I have found over many years that ERP can be summed up in the saying "less is more"—less thinking and more doing. It's about trusting life over fear to get your life back in balance.

Remember: OCD hates those of us who *trust* life over fear.

Helpful Words

Words have tremendous power to soothe an anxious brain. I use sticky notes on my bathroom mirror to help me remember what's true at any given moment. I also encourage you to create an "affirmation board" to have a collection of the same positive, motivating reminders. I've had one for years. Do whatever helps you.

Here are some mantras, prayers, and ideas that I have used to help calm, ground, and center myself before taking on any ERP. I encourage you to try them and use what works for you. They have worked for me.

The Serenity Prayer:
God, grant me the serenity to accept
the things I cannot change,
Courage to change the things I can,
And wisdom to know the difference.
~ Reinhold Niebuhr

Start by doing what is necessary, then do what's
possible, and suddenly you are doing the impossible.
~ St. Francis of Assisi

Never let a negative thought complete itself in your head.
~ Dr. Wayne Dyer

If a thought does not bring me inner
peace, I don't follow it.
~ Sharon Davies, OCD therapist

Here are some other affirmations and reassuring words that I use:

- "I choose to feel the feelings."
- "Every time I challenge it, I weaken it."
- "I choose to focus and trust."
- "If I think it might be OCD, it is."
- "I am not OCD. I am me."
- "I know the world does not work the way OCD wants me to think."
- "I choose to keep moving forward."
- "I choose progress not perfection."
- "I choose to slow it down and get mindful."
- "I choose to trust my body."
- "I choose to get conscious and present."
- "Regardless of what I see, think, or feel, keep going!"
- "I choose peace."

From my experience, it's crucial to remember that CBT/ERP is *about a willingness to make a commitment to feel good*. I often repeat the affirmation, "I want to feel good. And I'm committed to do whatever it takes."

According to *A Course in Miracles*, there are only two emotions—love and fear—and one cannot exist when the other is present. In my experience, love in all its forms clearly has an affect on my fears and works to calm them down. I have found that love from my family, friends, and myself is a powerful medicine.

I have learned to surrender to my feelings during my ERP work. Now, let me be clear on this: I am *not* surrendering to OCD but instead choosing to feel my feelings, and then letting them dissipate on their own. For me, it feels like

OCD loves a good fight but hates a good surrender. Let's face it. OCD fuels my Monkey Mind, which runs amok with "disaster-izing" and "catastrophe-izing."

So, how do I usually respond to this mess of OCD thoughts?

Repeat after me: "Thanks for sharing. I'm not caring." I say it out loud and in my mind to dissolve the obsessions: "Thanks for sharing OCD. But I'm not caring about your BS!"

I found out the hard way that *nothing changes if nothing changes.* It's true. ERP is work. And I have found it to be the toughest work of my life. But the payoff is simple: It gives me back my life.

Trust that: CBT and ERP can be trusted to work ... if you work them.

CHAPTER 14

Mindfulness: The Ultimate Anchor

Few of us ever live in the present. We are forever anticipating what is to come or remembering what has gone.

~ Louis L'Amour

After all of these years of analyzing, scrutinizing, and worrying about my own anxiety, I've come to the realization that I can trust the present moment. Trusting the moment has helped me learn to react to anxiety in a healthier way.

Since childhood, I've worried about the future—the "what ifs" in life:

- "What if I get sick?"
- "What if my family members get sick?"
- "What if I run out of money?"
- "What if I lose my job?"
- "What if I never find the right relationship?"
- "What if no treatment for OCD ever works for me?"
- "What if ...?"

The list was endless. And it put me in the "spin cycle," which boosted my anxiety and OCD symptoms into the stratosphere. I've attached a name to this "what if-ing" worrying process. And you won't find it in the dictionary. I call it "future-izing." In my opinion and experience, anxiety absolutely lives in the future. Let me repeat that: *Anxiety lives in the future.* It's deeply embedded and doesn't seem to want to let go. Whenever I began to obsess and worry about the "what ifs" of my life, a loved one's life, or any environmental or world issue, I was future-izing. And, while I hate labels, I have in the past labeled myself as a future-izer to remind myself to stop. But, of course, the stopping part wasn't so easy.

I defined the opposite side of the anxiety process like this: Whenever I started the "I could-ofs" or "I should-ofs," I became regretful and anxious:

- "I could've had a better job."
- "I should've communicated my feelings better."
- "I should've saved more money."
- "I could've behaved more like an adult."
- "I should've loved my wife more."
- "I could've made something of myself."
- "I should've lived a better life."

Nauseated yet? I am. The above examples, of course, would go on and on. And all I was doing was "shoulding" all over myself. I called this "pasteur-izing." You will find this word in the dictionary but with a much different definition. So, I was either future-izing or pasteur-izing, both unbelievably exhausting and disempowering to my spirit. I was either in anxiety mode or depression mode, or both.

I'm going to ask you to stretch your mind a little and open your heart to a new, yet very old, concept that I found useful when I caught myself slipping into anxious and depressing energy. Between the future (over which you have absolutely no control) and the past (over which you also have no control because it's gone) is a little moment called "the present." So, much of my life has been in a constant state of worry, or drowning in regret, guilt, shame, or anxiety. I completely missed the most important time—right now, this moment, *the present.*

In the present moment, if I were really honest with myself and trusted my feelings, I was okay. Let me be clear here: When I have anxiety, it hurts. It's painful. I'm not denying that at all. But worrying or future-izing about what that pain means, where it is going, or if it is going to get worse doesn't serve me in any way. Staying with the anxiety, being present with it, helps it move through me more quickly.

Mindfulness and Mindful Awareness

Living in the present moment is also called "mindfulness," which I have to work on all the time when doing ERP. It is a huge reminder that there's another way of thinking, another way of being. Just so you get the idea, here are a few good questions that I ask myself from time to time to help get more into the present moment:

- "When I eat dinner, do I really taste the food, or am I just gobbling it down?"
- "If I take a walk, am I truly seeing the beauty around me, feeling the air, hearing the sounds?"

For those of us with OCD, you don't have to take the details of mindfulness that far. For me, I'd rather call the process "mindful awareness"; that is, I catch myself moving out of the present moment. And that simple awareness shifts my consciousness a little to help bring me back to the here and now. That's it.

A good example is when I'm in OCD mode, and I'm washing my hands at the sink. Am I in the present moment, or am I imagining what may happen if I don't wash again and again and again? Just the awareness—that my washing over and over again is OCD at work—can lead me to take the risk to stop and feel all those feelings until they subside. And they do subside.

I found that mindful awareness is a practice that puts me more in the now, puts me in the present moment, and rewires my brain to handle anxiety better. Remember: Anxiety doesn't live in the present moment; it lives in the future.

You can think of mindful awareness as kind of an anchor for yourself. It is a practice that helps to anchor your thoughts to reality. When a boat is anchored, it stays in one place and does not drift.

Using Mindful Awareness to Stop Checking

Let me give you an example of how my anchors have worked for me while doing ERP work. Since the onset of my OCD in 1982, I've had an extremely annoying checking ritual when I walked, especially when I was alone. If it was a very stressful "OCD day," I walked down the street a few steps, and then went back to see if I stepped on anything—and "anything" was always nothing. From the day this checking ritual began in the '80s to the present day, I have never looked back and found anything that I stepped in or on that would be harmful to me in any way. *Ever.*

OCD gives meaning to meaningless things. That awareness is good. But I have experienced how OCD sabotages my thoughts and creates doubt. OCD is very creative. What if one day I "check" my steps along the way, and I *do* find something harmful to me but won't be able to handle it? This is why I needed a competent therapist or CBT/ERP coach to give me "anchors" for the irrational OCD thoughts. In other words, they would offer ways of looking at life differently or ways of acting differently than what OCD screamed at me. Remember how my wife Jeanine taught me how to take a shower differently? That was an anchor. I believe everyone with OCD has to be taught new anchors to shift their beliefs and actions. Now my job continues to be mindfully aware of these newly established anchors.

If I see an oil spot in the road that I've possibly stepped on, what does that mean in reality? It means that I stepped in a harmless, dried-up oil spot, of which there are many on any given street. However, if I'm not mindfully aware, or grounded in the present, OCD will give some kind of negative, distorted meaning to that meaningless oil spot. I would then shoot into the imagined future that this oil spot was laden with germs and contaminated and is now on my shoe. If I walk into my house, it will get on the floors where my wife will walk, and then she will pick up those germs and become sick, and ... so on and so on.

After many years, I got fed up with the "walking/checking ritual" and pushed myself to do ERP work every night for a summer, using the anchor my therapist gave me: "Just keep going. There's nothing that will harm me or others." I was instructed to walk with my head up while moving forward. My job was to be mindfully aware of that anchor as I walked. The objective was to be mindfully aware when OCD came in and tried to sabotage or twist reality.

My wife and I live along the northern California coast. We live in a nice neighborhood at the top of a hill, overlooking the ocean. If you walk up our street, you may just need a hit of oxygen because it's a very steep hill. I decided to walk down the hill each night and put ERP and mindful awareness to work. For some reason, walking downhill about a quarter of a mile was not that difficult. Walking back up, however, and needing to check for imaginary harm every few feet, were the challenges.

I distracted myself by listening to music or a book on my iPhone while walking. It wasn't just a distraction. But I was doing my best to be aware and mindful of being in the present moment with what I was hearing. I tried to focus on what was coming through the earpiece rather than buying into any OCD thoughts. It was not so easy at first, to be sure. But eventually my brain did habituate to a new way of thinking and acting. And I continue to practice this every time I take a walk. These days, though, I don't use the iPhone; rather, I try to be mindful of the beauty I'm seeing as I walk. I'm aware of OCD in the background of my mind. But I am more mindfully aware of the present moment. Most importantly, I become mindful of gratitude and appreciation of this beautiful spot that we call home. Checking has not been a problem for some time now.

Using Mindful Awareness to Let Go of Control

I have talked quite a bit about control in this book, as I believe and trust that the big picture of OCD recovery is all about letting go of control and living in the present moment. I will gladly take the calming feeling of the present moment over the controlling bullying of OCD any day.

Here are some reminders that I use to pull me out of "control mode" and into "present moment mode":

- "I have no control over what might happen."
- "I have no control over what did happen."

- "I have no control over other people's actions—only my own actions and reactions."
- "I do have control and choice about where I want to be in any given moment. I prefer the present moment."

Remember the desk that my brother made and where I hid all of my porn? The one that, at midnight, I found myself schlepping down my apartment stairs and hurling into the dumpster, trusting the instructions from my therapist Ron? Talk about freeing, about letting go of control. Talk about getting into the present and about empowerment. I felt it all. And it felt great!

I'm not suggesting that you start throwing out everything in your life. But consider letting go of some of the material things that keep you stuck in the past, especially if they harbor negative feelings that control you. Give them away to someone who truly needs them. It will help release you from the negative control of the past and feel good about living in the present. Work at letting go of all those negative thoughts attached to that past. Let go of the thoughts that once disempowered you. The past is the past. And living in the present is what mindfulness and mindful awareness are all about.

I practice mindfulness and living in the present, catching OCD thoughts about the future or past, and calming the symptoms of anxiety or depression before they take hold. It is not always easy. And I'm not always successful. But, when I am, catching those thoughts disarms OCD pretty fast. I've come to trust this more and more on a daily basis.

The Complainer

Here's another thought about being stuck in the past or future: "complaining." This word really made me laugh after the realization slapped me upside the head. Besides "the worrier," I've also been "the complainer." They can go hand in hand. And they have little to do with the present moment, even if the present moment isn't so great. Complaining begets more complaining. And on and on it goes.

One of my best friends, and one of the wonderful people to whom this book is dedicated, nagged me about complaining too much. We argued about it. But, in the end, he was right. I was complaining as an adult, just as I had been complaining as a child, and it was not serving me well in any way. In fact, complaining was only exacerbating my symptoms.

This situation came to light when I typed my name in an e-mail as "JimCallner" rather than "Jim Callner." Well, I spell checked "JimCallner," and what do you think spell check tossed back at me? The spell-check word correction for "JimCallner" was "Complainer." I kid you not. Talk about a wake-up call! When your computer is telling you to cut out the kvetching, that's bad!

The bottom line is that negative begets negative, and complaining begets complaining. The less I do it, the better I feel. And the better people around me feel. That kind of energy is what I want for my healing and recovery from OCD. Take *that*, spell check!

Trust that: Being mindfully aware and living in the present moment are choices. In truth, the present is the only time we really have. Each moment of your life is a gift. That's why it's called "the present." Trust this wisdom from Louise Hay: "The point of power is always in the present moment."

CHAPTER 15

Love Heals

*Too often we underestimate the power
of a touch, a smile, a kind word, a
listening ear, an honest compliment, or
the smallest act of caring, all of which
have the potential to turn a life around.*

~ Leo F. Buscaglia

The strength of love has the power to heal family, friends, coworkers, acquaintances, and, in turn, the world.

Love heals. I wish I had known and fully understood the impact of these words when the onset of OCD came into my life. Early on, those two words could have been the impetus for teaching family and friends how to best treat me. And, equally as important, how they needed to be treated. OCD didn't just hit me; it hit my entire family.

As in most life struggles, it was a two-way street. Everyone in my life who hung in there with me was willing to stay open to all healing possibilities, including compassion, patience, appreciation, gratitude, and especially love. I too had to be open and reciprocate in equal measures, offering them the same understanding and kindness they gave me. I felt the most support and love from those who could "see me" and "love me" for who and what I was, beyond the OCD.

However, life isn't always that simple. And an easy flow of understanding and compassion was not always the case. There was resistance on both parts. You know, when someone gets sick in the family, some family members want to try and fix them, heal them, and take that sickness away quickly. Their intentions are good. But they may be giving suggestions without understanding the problem. They may give advice before asking whether or not that person wants advice because they are so desperate to see them whole again.

Years ago, Phil offered a bit of wisdom, or insight, that I never forgot: "Never give information to someone that isn't useful." This is a simple concept and a wonderful reminder about thinking twice before putting something out there. Oftentimes, pausing, thinking things through, and rewording in a more mindful way can bypass misunderstanding, hurt, or even unintentional guilt or shame.

I needed to catch myself all the time with family and friends. I equate it to telling someone, *"You should* quit smoking" or *"You need to* lose some weight." I mean, seriously, don't you think they know that? It is useless information for the person who already knows and struggles with these extremely hard challenges. Instead of being helpful, it is hurtful. It is all about how we word things. Pressing the pause button, or simply changing a single word, can turn words that could be harsh and painful into words of caring and compassion. We all must find ways to be less judgmental and accept those who are dealing with crises, whether or not we understand the struggle.

Here are a few examples of "information" that I received over the years that were never very useful to me and to which I wanted to reply, "Ya think?" Cynical, yes. But, at the same time, these bits of "information" hurt more than they helped and frustrated me:

- "You should stop washing your hands." ("Ya think?")
- "You need to be on time." ("Ya think?")
- "You could stop if you worked harder." ("Ya think?")

They may have meant well. And yes, the above comments were more than likely made from concern. With a little mindful shifting, what could cause hurt and shame could be turned into helpful and loving support. Below is a more compassionate approach with examples of how rewording can be healing. From my experience, these word "shifts" create more loving and supportive statements:

- "You should stop washing your hands" can be shifted to "Are you willing to let me help you stop washing with some ERP coaching?"
- "You need to be on time" can be shifted to "I know it's a challenge to be on time because the OCD rituals hold on tightly. But let me help you help yourself."
- "You could stop if you worked harder" can be shifted to "I have faith and trust in you that you can do this. Let's take it one day at a time, one moment at a time. I'm on your side."

These "shift" statements feel supportive. They are softer, more compassionate, loving, and empowering. These shifted statements feel as though my family and friends are not only with me but are now "seeing me," without judgment or shame.

So, what other words are useful for someone with OCD?

- "How can I help support you?"
- "Let's both learn what this disorder is and how it really works."
- "You're not alone on this, even if I don't understand it right now."
- "When the chips are down, and you are struggling, I will do my best to be there for you with my actions, not just my words."
- "I believe you. And I'm going to remind you that you are not OCD. You are you."

- "You are not crazy. You are dealing with a neurobiological illness."
- "I love and accept you, no matter what."

And here are very important words I ask of others and of myself: "I need you to tell me I'm okay, even for the smallest accomplishment."

Let me stress that dealing with OCD, for both the person diagnosed and for those in their lives, is a learning process. I encourage everyone to let go of the need to be right, and choose kindness and compassion. Remember: You are not fighting the person; you are fighting the OCD.

There Are Only Two Emotions: Love and Fear

My grandmother used to say, "Schmear people with love."

This is a Yiddish word, and much of Yiddish is kind of untranslatable into English. Just think of it like schmearing a bagel with cream cheese, even though people are not bagels. But, boy, do we love to schmear cream cheese! So, "schmearing people with love" would translate to "Give love unconditionally with happiness and joy." My grandmother was good at that. The "schmearing process" enabled my grandmother to give love and gifted her with a huge dose of love in return. When you give love, you get love. Clear and simple.

As I've mentioned many times, I am not a religious person. But I am always open to a religion or belief system that helps soothe an anxious mind. I have studied many philosophies in order to keep my mind open to all possibilities, as finding solace and a peaceful place is first and foremost. Here are some of the teachings and philosophies that have helped me come back to love in times of fear.

Helpful Philosophies

In my quest, I only dabbled in *A Course in Miracles*, as some of the language didn't resonate with me. But many of the ideas did. For example, "Your safety lies in truth and not in lies. Love is your safety." *A Course in Miracles* goes on to say that "love casts out fear." I choose to interpret this as "when love is present, fear cannot exist" and vice versa. I focus very hard on love in my recovery, which is one of the main messages in *A Course in Miracles*: "There are only two emotions: love and fear." And, in my experience, OCD is all about fear. To counter those OCD fears, I need to find a place of love.

How do I get to that place of love? The quickest way for me is to focus on gratitude and appreciation for simple things: "I ate today; I got out of bed today; I can breathe, walk, talk, see ..." (Nature is also a huge way to calm my anxious mind.)

Lao Tzu was a Chinese philosopher, who wrote the *Tao Te Ching* (The Great Way) in the late fourth century BC. His spiritual wisdom is eternal. Here are a few of his quotes that I love:

- "Being deeply loved by someone gives you strength, while loving someone deeply gives you courage."
- "Kindness in words creates confidence. Kindness in thinking creates profoundness. Kindness in giving creates love."

- "Because of a great love, one is courageous."
- "Love is of all passions the strongest, for it attacks simultaneously the head, the heart and the senses."

The 14th Dalai Lama talks about love with a simple quote: "Love and compassion are necessities, not luxuries. Without them humanity cannot survive."

Mother Teresa on love said, "If we really want to love we must learn how to forgive."

And Saint Francis of Assisi, in *The Little Flowers of St. Francis of Assisi,* wrote, "All the darkness in the world cannot extinguish the light of a single candle." I believe the candle not only represents light but also a loving light of calmness and peace.

Finally, one of my favorite contemporary authors and teachers—Eckhart Tolle—has many quotes that soothe me:

- "To love is to recognize yourself in another."
- "Sometimes letting things go is an act of far greater power than defending or hanging on."
- "This, too, will pass."

Many philosophers, poets, healers, and medical doctors around the world have talked about love and its healing powers. How do I know that love has such profound healing powers? I've experienced it from the love of my wife, friends, and family, and from extended family including OCD support groups, 12-step groups, and by simply reading and listening to inspiring words about love and how to love yourself again.

Affirmations and quotes like the ones above have helped me to shift from feeling anxious, cynical, depressed, and hopeless to the beginnings of peace and hope. From this,

I have found that the more I've allowed myself to feel that peace and hope, the more I can give and receive love.

Choosing, and working, to shift my fears to a place of love and gratitude have truly helped me through the years.

It is not always easy. And it does take time. For me to shift into self-love, I start with a "gratitude list." However, instead of writing a list, I simply lie in bed at night and quietly think of as many things as I can that I am grateful for, in no particular order. The more items on my mental list, the better. It does have a profound effect of quieting my mind. It goes something like this:

"I'm grateful that I'm breathing. I'm grateful that my anxiety is lower. I'm grateful that I'm lying in bed. I'm grateful that I have a bed. I'm grateful that I can walk and that I can move. I'm grateful that there is some treatment for OCD and that I'm taking some action toward my recovery. I'm grateful for the beautiful day today, and the quiet of the night. I'm grateful for online support groups because I can always connect with other people with OCD who understand. I'm grateful for any and all help. I'm grateful that I heard music today. I'm grateful for my home and my wife. I'm grateful for my friends. I'm grateful that I can choose to calm myself. I'm grateful that I have a creative mind. I'm grateful that I know I'm bigger than OCD and know I can manage it—one day at a time. I'm grateful that I know deep down that love always conquers fear. I'm grateful to be alive. And I know that I'll continue to get better and better and better ..."

But listen, don't overthink this love thing! Try it. Just try to live each moment in a loving state. And do the best you can. Some days will be easier than others. And that's okay.

- When you have a choice between love and fear, always choose love.
- When you have a choice between cynicism and understanding, always choose understanding.
- When you have a choice between complaining and gratitude, always choose gratitude.
- When you have a choice between self-hatred and self-love, always choose self-love.
- And when you have a choice between an OCD thought and the quiet voice of reason within all of us, choose the quiet voice of reason because it's the voice you can always trust.

The bottom line is this: What I have come to know, without a doubt, is that *love can help heal and give you peace from OCD.*

Larry's Love

This section is based on a true story that happened to me in the 1990s. After I finished directing *The Touching Tree* and it was released, I got a phone call from a father whose son Larry wanted desperately to meet me. Larry found out that he and I lived in the same town. His father explained to me that Larry had severe OCD but still wanted to meet me.

Larry had the worse case of OCD that I had ever seen. He was housebound and had essentially lived in one chair, located in the center of the family's living room, for two years. He did not eat but drank only one flavor of a protein drink—blueberry. I was surprised that he was not hospitalized and was still alive. How he went to the bathroom, or if he showered, is still a mystery to me.

I showed up one night at Larry's door with a friend to meet this challenged teenager. I remember that it was a warm, summer night when Larry's father opened the door. Through the screen, I could see a thin, teenage boy, sitting quietly in a recliner in the middle of the room with only a towel over his lap.

Larry's father greeted me. "Would you mind taking off your shoes, Mr. Callner?"

My anxiety slowly building, I looked at the father and calmly said, "Well, we have a problem here. I really want to meet your son Larry. But I don't take off my shoes in other people's homes. I have OCD too, you know."

Then I called out to Larry from outside the door. "I'm here, Larry. And I really want to meet you. But I won't take off my shoes to come in your house. So, you'll have to trust me and take the risk that there's nothing on my shoes or my friend's shoes that can harm you or anybody. Okay?"

The father turned around and looked at Larry for an answer. Maybe for the first time, he was giving Larry the power to make his own decisions. Larry didn't think too long, and the door opened. We went in and sat down on a couch, about three feet away. The first thing I noticed was the obvious: how pale, grey, and malnourished he looked, as all he was surviving on was the blueberry protein drink.

I also noticed the paintings, which Larry had created, hanging on the walls around his chair. I asked him if he was an artist. He shyly said yes and showed me some of his work. I must say that, in all the years of meeting people challenged by OCD, I have never met anyone who was not creative, artistic, articulate, and highly self-aware. *Never.* We talked awhile about movies, art, and our mutual struggles with OCD. We talked about *The Touching Tree* and how difficult it was for me to direct the film, even though I had OCD, and about how I got through it with the help of many people who worked on the movie.

I moved my attention to his art on the walls and his talent. I mean, how could he draw such incredible paintings in the midst of such pain? It amazed me. They were all wonderful drawings. We then talked about how painful OCD was for both of us—the pain of obsessions we both had about germs and contamination.

I left the house, thinking about what a great kid Larry was and how, in my view, his family loved him but were unconsciously enabling him. Let's face it. Their lives seemed to revolve around Larry's chair. As tough as this opinion might sound, I felt that OCD was literally the center of the family's life. Meeting Larry was a powerful experience. And my hopes and prayers were that he would someday be able to free himself from the bondage of OCD—and that chair.

About a year later, I was premiering a new movie that I had made about OCD called *The Risk.* The premier was held at the college theater where I was working. After the showing of the movie, a crowd formed around me to ask questions, or shake my hand, or thank me. I'm always a little uncomfortable with this. But, at the same time, I am grateful and humbled by it.

This night, my gratitude shot into the stratosphere. As people congratulated me on the film, I felt a tap on my shoulder. I turned around and, in a full suit and tie, Larry was standing next to me. I couldn't believe it!

"Larry, what are you *doing* here? You're supposed to be stuck in a chair!"

Larry smiled and simply said, "I'm getting better."

As I could see, and as I believe did Larry, he was not only getting better by leaps and bounds but was on his way to recovery. I knew the therapist who worked with Larry but had no idea of the details of his recovery nor of how his family stopped the enabling and began loving him all the more. All I knew was that I had witnessed the worst case of OCD I had ever seen and now saw in front of me the vision of what hope, recovery, and love looked like: a teenage boy, standing in front of me in a suit and tie, smiling, and quietly saying, "I'm getting better."

I Choose Love

The mantra Phil gave me in the 1980s was "I choose peace." I use it all the time when I'm stuck or anxious. It affirms my intentions for peace in both mind and body. And I believe the power of these words connects you to an even deeper inner strength. I encourage you to use "I choose love" as well, as these mantras or affirmations will help you heal, if you use and trust them.

As schmaltzy as it sounds, we came into this world as love. And it's still there, embedded in us forever, if we consciously and steadfastly stay connected with it. It means that we have to work at catching ourselves at being judgmental and shaming, blaming, or criticizing ourselves or others. It's a moment-to-moment exercise for me. But I know that, deep down and on all levels imaginable, love heals.

Think about these questions:

- "Is there a better way to help someone's anxiety than through love?"
- "Is there a better way to soothe an anxious mind than through the stillness of loving thoughts?"
- "Is there a better way to receive love than by giving love?"

The answer to all of these questions is, "Love is the most powerful, positive, and transformative way."

I wrote about my mother's passing in this book. She and I had many talks by phone and Skype. I remember that, one night, she was very anxious and nauseous. She called, and I tried my best to soothe her with love. I told her what I did for my nausea, which was to take ginger in any form. She had some ginger tea available, so she was able to stop the nausea quickly. Then, I encouraged her to take an antianxiety medication that her doctors prescribed as needed. My mother was unsure. But it was exactly what I would do, and I told her so. She took the medication while I was on the phone with her. And I told her that I would stay with her until the medication started to work. I told her that it should only take about 20 minutes to get into her bloodstream.

Softly, I did my best to calm her down and talk about how all would be well in a few minutes, and how amazing that a natural substance like ginger could take nausea away. I believed it was the adrenaline from her anxiety that caused her nausea. And I told my mother that now she had a remedy to use. I use it often for digestion in capsule form.

All this soothing, loving talk calmed my mother down. As the medication took effect, we talked about how that was also a tool she could use for anxiety. You see, connecting, loving, soothing, soft talk, and staying with the person makes the difference. I will never forget that night and many others.

So, here's the bottom line about all this love stuff. Here's what I had to understand and bring myself to do, and to work at, if I really wanted to heal:

- I have lost friends who just couldn't grasp the idea that OCD was real. I needed to let them go but love them anyway—*if I wanted to heal.*

- Members of my family have been frustrated and angry with the OCD and me. I needed to see that some of them just didn't have the capacity or were too fearful to understand. My job was not to blame or shame them, for that would be counterproductive to healing. Loving them for who they are is the objective—*if I wanted to heal.*

- I have had coworkers and friends who have made fun of me or have been unwilling to "get it." I needed to love them by setting my own boundaries around interacting with them—*if I wanted to heal.*

- I have shamed, blamed, criticized, and judged myself endlessly. But I had to work to let the past go and live fully in the present, living in each moment—*if I truly wanted to heal.*

Is love the answer to everything?

I say, "Yes."

OCD has caused me enough pain, so I choose not to doubt but to embrace and gracefully allow love into my life. Accept it, hold it, and return it.

Trust that: Love heals.

CHAPTER 16

What Really
Helped Me?

*Start by doing what's necessary; then
do what's possible; and suddenly
you are doing the impossible.*

~ St. Francis of Assisi

Phil and Ron decided to retire around 2007. I had been receiving treatment and wisdom from Phil since the time of my breakdown in 1982; Ron joined the team shortly thereafter. It never occurred to me that they would retire. I mean, seriously, I thought we would go on forever. But, deep down, I knew there was no "forever," with the exception of the love they gave to me and the wisdom I received, which I now share with others challenged with OCD. I'm grateful to say that I still keep in touch with these incredible men who both played such a vital role in my recovery.

I was left, however, with the challenge of finding a new duo, as I liked the team approach, always reassured that if one therapist was out of town, the other was available. I liked backup.

The hunt to match Phil and Ron was virtually impossible. As so many of us know, "shopping" for a therapist who is knowledgeable about OCD and has the right level of compassion is not easy. The hard fact I came across was that there just aren't enough psychiatrists or therapists who are really trained to help those of us with OCD. It took me five years to find a therapist who knew enough about OCD and who could offer knowledge, wisdom, compassion, and trust.

The first therapist I chose did not know as much about OCD as I would have liked but was open and willing to learn about me, which was and is crucial to my ongoing recovery. With that component of her personality, I found the trust I needed and signed her up.

The second and main therapist came into my life synchronistically. I am part of nine different private OCD support group pages on Facebook. Sharon Davies, OCD therapist and the Director of The OCD Treatment Centre in England, became Facebook "friends" with me. Sharon was asking for some of my thoughts and opinions about specific OCD symptoms. We messaged each other back and forth for some time before it hit me like a ton of bricks: "Why don't I ask Sharon if she would be my therapist?" She knew more about OCD than anyone I'd ever met simply because she had been challenged with it herself and knew from firsthand experience. Sharon and I shared the same sensibilities and spirituality that made us a great match.

I work with both of these compassionate people to this day. I am blessed to have these champions on my side.

So, what really helped in my ongoing recovery from OCD? There were many components. But the core ideas, treatments, and help came from the following areas. I work on one or more of these every day. I hope some will resonate with you too.

Can You Laugh at OCD?

If you have gotten this far in the book, you know that I'm pretty big on trust, compassion, and love. I honestly believe that these values were my greatest teachers. Oh, and there was one more seriously important teacher that I needed to embrace: *laughter.* Yes, I said laughter. How do you find humor in OCD? Is it okay to laugh at OCD? Is it okay to laugh at yourself?

The answer is a resounding "Yes."

But, in my opinion, there is one condition: Don't laugh at my struggles or at me. That's called bullying. Did you get that one? *Don't bully me by laughing at my disorder.* You can laugh *with* me but not *at* me. And, as with anyone's personal struggles, laughing *with* but not *at* is a boundary we should all embrace. It's all about respect and common sense. There are moments with OCD—or any other illness or disorder—when the depth of pain or anxiety is so great that it's often indescribable. To laugh at one's struggle is ignorant, insensitive, and cruel.

As I've often said in this book, OCD really loves the dark and hates the light. (Sounds a bit like a Dracula movie!) But the truth is that, when I'm caught up or buried in obsessions and/or rituals, I can't help but feel trapped in a very dark and frightening place. At those moments, I must remember that one of the answers to shifting out of the darkness and breaking the obsessions and compulsions is introducing a bit of lightness.

I used to go into Ron's office overwhelmed with anxiety and fear. I'd sit on his couch, ready to spill my guts of panic, when he would say, "Before we get started, I just have to tell you about a movie I saw last night. It was so funny, Jim. If you get a chance to see this film ..."

See what he was doing? He was so in tune with my level of anxiety and darkness that, before I even began, he introduced the light, breaking the OCD for that moment. And it worked. The simple technique of shifting the focus from one of darkness to light was a distraction that helped ease my anxiety.

Bringing light into the shower ritual, however, has been a work in progress. These days, I still have trouble ritualizing in the shower. I work with my wife as my ERP coach, as a family member can be a coach if they are willing. Jeanine helps me. But, if I'm stuck in the middle of a washing ritual—let's say washing one leg over and over again—Jeanine will burst into song: "Rollin', rollin', rollin'... keep them doggies rollin'... Rawhide!" Soapy and sopping wet, I start to smile and something shifts. Is she laughing at me? No. She's reminding me to keep it light, bringing me out of the darkness. Or maybe she's hinting that, if I keep on scrubbin', I'll end up with a "raw hide." Either way, she makes me smile.

Here's how I think about OCD after dealing with it for so many years: I take OCD seriously. But I can't afford to take myself too seriously. I believe in the healing power of laughter as a treatment for OCD as well as for all disorders and diseases.

Norman Cousins, the journalist and author who wrote the famous book, *Anatomy of an Illness: As Perceived by the Patient,* describes how, after he was diagnosed with a life-threatening form of arthritis, he decided to watch Marx Brothers movies and other comedies that essentially made him laugh into recovery. He subscribed to the belief of "healing through laughter."

I subscribe and trust this method of healing because laughter has been a huge part of my life. And it always— and I mean *always*—distracts and refocuses my brain for the better. So, sometimes we have to somehow find a way to laugh through our pain to gain relief.

Can you laugh at OCD? In my opinion, the questions and answers are clear.

Can you laugh to help heal yourself from OCD? Yes! No question.

Should you laugh *at* someone with OCD? No!

Can you laugh *with* someone with OCD without labeling? Absolutely.

"Don't Label Me!"

> *Once you label me, you negate me.*
> ~ Søren Kierkegaard

In seventh grade, I had a friend named Chris. He was a precocious kid, full of talent and ambition. In my youth, my father and I even made a short movie with him. One day, seemingly out of nowhere, Chris came up to me on the playground and said, "You Jew!" (I can remember the exact spot at Blackford Junior High.)

To this day, I don't know where that came from. And it's still scripted in my mind. That's over 50 years ago: "You Jew."

What was I supposed to *do* with that? I was not a fighter. And I am Jewish. While I was not brought up in a very religious household, I knew I was Jewish. His voice was the voice of an angry, prejudiced bully.

I must have just walked away.

But, that night, you know what I did? I called him and tried to make friends with him. Can you believe it? After all, we had been friends before. I tried to no avail. Wrong move. But I was in seventh grade and had no real knowledge of what bigotry meant.

I have no idea where Chris is today. And, although I have never forgotten his words, I have forgiven him. I've found forgiveness to be the only way to heal and move forward. My guess is that his name-calling, labeling, and bigotry in that moment long ago came from a child who most likely learned this hatred from his parents.

To this day, and with all of my life experiences and my many years of education, what I still remember most vividly was Chris standing next to me on that playground and saying, in the angriest, most derogatory way, "You Jew."

For me, the same applies to OCD. Calling someone with OCD a "germaphobe," "crazy," "psycho," "clean freak," "weird," or any of the other derogatory terms is painful and can be scripted into minds forever. Words hurt. That hurt can scar, whether from a stranger, a family member, or a once-trusted friend.

The bottom line to this one is very simple: It's true that, once you label someone, you negate them. *Don't do it!*

Teachers of Spirituality

Now hold it! I've said it before, and I'll say it again: For those of you who are challenged with OCD and uncomfortable with religion, I'm not using the word "spirituality" in the religious context here. Not at all, so relax. That said, if religion helps you in any way, stay with it. I believe that whatever works for you—and doesn't hurt you—is worth making part of your life.

My own meaning for the word "spiritual" is "healing a broken spirit." When I was in TC-1 with raging OCD symptoms, my spirit—or the funny, energetic, positive, spirited Jim—was broken. In other words, nothing was funny or positive during that time. It felt like my spirit, soul, and higher self had left me. I was in pain, clear and simple. I was in pain. And I hurt bad.

I am now aware that my spirit never really left me but was clearly damaged, wounded, and in need of repair. Since then, I have been on a journey to heal and put my spirit back together. Learning about spirituality, or healing my wounded spirit, became my job. For me, spirituality meant keeping my mind open to all possibilities.

As Phil used to say, "Jim, you just need to stay in spiritual gear." To me, this meant getting back into trusting my higher self, the part of me that intuitively knows what is true, what is real, and what I can trust.

Around 1987, I started going to 12-step programs and some conferences that featured Dr. Wayne Dyer, Pia Mellody, Bob Earle, Melody Beattie, and a host of other people who are key teachers of self-help wisdom. Are they gurus? No. They are spiritual teachers and authors of books and materials that can help you find yourself again and help you live with more peace than fear and anxiety. This interested me. These spiritual teachers write and talk about their own struggles, how they work to get past them, and the tools I can use to help my own challenges with anxiety, panic, and depression, all of which I've experienced with OCD.

As I have said, it is my belief that OCD robs you of trust. Therefore, for me, it seemingly also robbed me of who I was and how I was supposed to *be* in life. As I opened myself up to the teachings, I gradually reclaimed a belief in trusting life, in trusting humanity, and in trusting myself—all rooted in appreciation, compassion, and love. This felt a lot better than any false, fear-based belief system that OCD offered.

Does that sound too "new agey"? I can tell you that it's "*old* agey"—full of simplicity, common sense, and more love than you could ever imagine.

Remember that love heals. And being in some kind of "spiritual gear" or awareness of higher self or power (or whatever you may choose to call it) simply feels good ... and good is where I prefer to be. In fact, feeling good is more important than anything in my life. Check out some of the teachers whom I have read, listened to, or watched every day to get my dose of feeling good.

In his book, *The Way of the Wizard: Twenty Spiritual Lessons for Creating the Life You Want*, Deepak Chopra, MD, wrote, "In the light of trust, as it develops slowly over time, you will find that you are a privileged child of the universe, entirely safe, entirely supported, entirely loved."

This is my goal: To feel safe and loved by others and by my inner self. For me, it happens when I focus on something other than OCD. Let me rephrase that: *When OCD offers me thoughts of fear and doom, I choose to refocus on some of the wisdom from spiritual teachers.*

Louise Hay, author and speaker, is one of my favorite teachers and one of the founders of the self-help movement. In her article, "You Are an Infinite Treasure: Know it and live it!" from healyourlife.com, she wrote, "Remember, many questions we may have about life are beyond our current understanding. That's part of our spiritual learning, to continually expand our understanding of this magnificent experience called Life, ... It's our personalities that need to be reminded that we're spiritual beings having a human experience, not the other way around. As we grow spiritually, we see the perfection of all life." Ah, great point! It's our personalities that need reminding that we are spiritual beings having a human experience. This I like.

Dr. Wayne Dyer, a spiritual teacher of inspiration and motivation, and one of my greatest teachers through his books, CDs, and lectures, wrote these important words: "Never let a negative thought complete itself in your head." This one is so important to me because it validates my practice of not following an OCD thought. When one comes up—and they often do during my waking day—I become aware of it, label it as OCD, and choose not to follow the thought. Is this easy? Of course not. It takes lots and lots of practice. But it really works for me.

Melody Beattie, another one of my favorite teachers and the best-selling author of *The Language of Letting Go: Daily Meditations for Codependents*, wrote "Today I will ask God to help me let go of my need to be afraid. I welcome peace, trust, acceptance, and safety into my life. I will make a point of listening to my healthy, rational fears, and will relinquish all the others." I keep this book on the kitchen table and often read a page or two—just to remind myself of the truth.

I have never been afraid of the word "God." For me, it means my higher self, love, nonjudgment, and trust. It's hard to explain. But it kinda feels like some kind of inner companion that, when I am at my worst, seems to give me some sense of the larger perspective by reminding me, "It's really not worth all this drama, Jim. You are just fine."

As I've mentioned, if the word "God" makes you feel uncomfortable in any way, then I suggest replacing it with the word "love," "goddess," "source," "universe," "Yahweh," "creator," or "peace." To me, it doesn't matter what you call it; all that matters is that you believe in something, and that something is a part of you and everything else.

Mindfulness and focusing on the present moment is vital for OCD recovery and balanced living. Eckhart Tolle, author of *The Power of Now: A Guide to Spiritual Enlightenment* and *Stillness Speaks*, taught me the most about being in the moment: "Not to be able to stop thinking is a dreadful affliction. But we don't realize this because almost everyone is suffering from it, so it is considered normal. This incessant mental noise prevents you from finding that realm of inner stillness that is inseparable from Being." The practice of mindfulness has been an essential tool for me in calming my anxiety and in coming back to the present moment.

Leo Buscaglia, the teacher who started me on this spiritual journey through his PBS shows in the 1980s, wrote many books including *Love: What Life Is All About*, *Personhood*, and *Living, Loving & Learning*. He once said,

"There are two big forces at work, external and internal. We have very little control over external forces such as tornadoes, earthquakes, floods, disasters, illness, and pain. What really matters is the internal force. <u>How do I respond to those disasters? Over that I have complete control</u>." *respond and*

We have control over how we think and *react*. That means a lot to me in recovery from OCD. I learned many years ago, however, that we also have no control over how others think, feel, or act. Therefore, when OCD hits me with "magical thinking" that I have some control over others through my bad thoughts, which could prove harmful to them, I need to trust that it is simply untrue.

I love what His Holiness the 14th Dalai Lama, spiritual leader of Tibet, teaches on compassion: "Compassion is not religious business, it is human business, it is not luxury, it is essential for our own peace and mental stability, it is essential for human survival." He also teaches, "Love and compassion are necessities, not luxuries. Without them, humanity cannot survive."

I remember seeing the Dalai Lama with my wife at a huge outdoor arena with some 20,000 people. We were fortunate to have seats in the front section, so we could be a bit closer to the stage where he was sitting in a chair with his interpreter next to him. As I looked back on this sea of humanity, I heard nothing. I mean *nothing*. It was silent. I had been to concerts at that outdoor arena that were so loud you couldn't hear your own thoughts. That day, however, 20,000 people were in respectful silence. Through his interpreter, he answered questions from the audience.

One question that hit me in the heart was, "What makes you happy?"

The Dalai Lama thought for a second and seemed stumped. He just couldn't answer. So he started to laugh.

As I study this man of love and compassion, I like to believe that he was stumped on that happiness question because he knows that nothing can make you happy. Happiness is within. You make yourself happy.

Maybe that's why he just laughed.

Do I believe every word from these spiritual teachers and others? Of course not. No one man or woman has all the answers to life's questions. I do trust and resonate with enough of the wonderful teachings to believe them. And this makes me feel good, which helps me shift from anxiety to calmness.

For me, it's not hard to set aside time each day to read a sentence or paragraph, listen to a CD, or watch some of the people whom I've mentioned to help reset my thinking and move from anxiety to a happier, more hopeful state. It is truly worth the effort. By refocusing and shifting my attention away from me and OCD, it allows room for something soothing into my life: moments of peace.

Simple Breathing Meditation

I remember when Jeanine and I were dating. During the summers, Jeanine would take off to Greece to teach Reiki and energy healing to a special women's group. One year, Jeanine seemed to be on the fence about our relationship—

not that she wanted to end it. But she was unsure of its future.

Now, you have to remember that virtually, from the beginning, I had "a knowing" about this woman, that she was *the one for me*. But hearing of her uncertainty threw me into a state of high anxiety, which, on a scale of 1 to 10, was an 18. The thought of her leaving me was overwhelming. There was no way to resolve her feelings about "being on the fence" regarding our relationship before she had to leave for Greece. So, off she went, leaving me worried and anxious, obsessing about "what if?" These thoughts exacerbated several physical symptoms and OCD.

What to do?

Well, I did the usual talk therapy with Phil and Ron, which helped tremendously during this time of crisis. And I discovered The Center for Integrative Medicine in San Jose, California. This holistic center offered a variety of therapeutic options, including acupuncture, yoga, mindfulness, and holistic treatments for well-being.

One nurse practitioner, whom I saw many times, was highly trained in the art of meditation. I had never learned or practiced meditation. And, quite frankly, I was somewhat skeptical of how powerful it could be. Could it truly be that beneficial to my nervous system, my entire mind and body? There are many ways to meditate. And you can find books, CDs, DVDs, and all kinds and variations of meditation practices. But I learned the most basic form from this wonderful nurse and friend, and this is what I want to share with you. I'm going to give you the abbreviated version of my meditation experience, which I believe can work for anyone.

It is based on what my teacher said to me. Her name was Deborah, and she simply said this:

"Now you are sitting very straight in your chair with your hands comfortably resting on your thighs. You are in a very dignified position. And your eyes are closed. But you're fully awake. You're breathing normally and easily. Breathe in through your nose, in and out. Again, easily, inhale through your nose, and easily exhale through your nose. I want you to put all your attention on the breath. Focus on the air going in and the air going out ... the air going in and going out. There's no need to force anything. But simply put all your attention and awareness on the breath. Breathe normally and feel the air as you inhale going in and as you exhale easily going out. All your awareness is on the breath."

As Deborah softly spoke her directions, I could feel my body start to relax. But my mind was a problem. I kept having racing thoughts. And it was hard to focus only on my breath.

Then, Deborah said, "It's completely natural to have thoughts come into your consciousness. Simply and gently notice them, name them, and let them go. Notice them, name them, and let them go. And come back to the breath."

What this meant to me was that I needed to become aware of my thoughts but not let them complete themselves in my head. Instead, I would interrupt the thought and bring my focus back to my breath going in and out. I would imagine the thought being shot into space, beaming it out of my mind. This inner visual or thought helped me through the hundreds, if not thousands, of thoughts that came in. The challenge was to continually come back to the breath.

Deborah continued. "It's completely natural to have thoughts coming into your mind. Just notice them, name them, let them go, and come back to breath. Be present with the breath."

This word "present" or "being in the now" with my breath was vitally important in calming me down. Be present, not past, not future, but right now—in this moment.

After some practice, I found myself better able to focus on my breath and the air going in and out. And a feeling of calmness came over me. Deborah emphasized that, even though my eyes were shut, I was fully awake and aware.

She ended my guided meditation, saying, "I want you to think of one thing, just one thing that you're grateful for today."

I was grateful that this practice of just breathing, focusing, and being aware was able to bring a halt to my anxiety. I was surprised to find that this simple breathing meditation could bring my anxiety down so quickly. The difficult part for me was mastering the discipline.

Some experts suggest that you meditate twice a day for 20 minutes; however, others say that any time given to meditation, no matter how little, is beneficial to body and mind. This means that you can do it for one minute or five minutes—whatever you can do will help.

What I've learned from my own meditation experience, with or without the special meditation tape that Deborah created for me, is that it helps me feel less anxious. I feel an overwhelming sense of calmness and groundedness, hope, and the sense that I will be okay.

You can record your own meditation tape. Just use Deborah's words above.

Jeanine returned from Greece that summer with a ring for me that she had bought there. I'm not sure what happened on those beautiful islands. But thankfully she decided to come back to our relationship. Four years later, we got married and have been learning and loving ever since.

And I continue to meditate whenever I can.

Medications and Supplements

This is a small section on how medications and supplements have helped me in my ongoing recovery with OCD. You should check all medications and supplements with a qualified medical health professional.

I was chairing a 12-step meeting many years ago and, after the meeting, a man named George came up to talk to me. He seemed very awkward and shy, so I took the initiative. And the conversation went something like this:

Jim: "Hi. How are you doing?"

George: "I've wanted to talk to you. But I've been a little scared too."

Jim: "I understand. I'm scared most of the time. So, what's going on?"

George: "You talked in the meeting about OCD."

Jim: "Yep, I have OCD. And this 12-step stuff really helps."

George: "You said you take medication for the OCD."

Jim: "Absolutely. That really helps too. You don't have to answer this but do you have OCD too?"

George: "Yes. And I'm afraid to take medication because I think it will change my personality."

Jim: "I understand the fear. My opinion and experience is that the medication doesn't change your personality. But the OCD sure makes you horribly anxious. True?"

George: "Yes, it's true."

Jim: "So, the way I see it is that OCD is a biological disorder. And medication can bring me back into balance by reducing the anxiety and help me to restore my true spirit. Know what I mean?"

George: "I understand what you're saying. But I'm so scared. I mean, which one do you take?"

Jim: "Well, that question I can relate to big time. I personally take a prescribed amount of antianxiety medication and stay on that amount to manage my anxiety. Then I work very hard on ERP. That's the plan that my psychiatrist has set up for me. But everyone is different. I look at medication as just another tool to help my anxiety. I have tried several other medications to see if there is anything else that works with my system. So, if you find a medication that helps, and it's okay with your doc, then I say go for it. You might not need to stay on meds all your life. But I don't think you have to suffer! I have not experienced any change in my personality other than it helped bring down my anxiety, so I could move on to the work of ERP."

As it turned out, I became very good friends with George. And we even shared the same psychiatrist for some time.

Keep this in mind: Medication is a tricky business as every "body" is different and reacts differently. That said, and as you know, I am not against medication in addition to therapy and CBT/ERP work.

Personally, I have also found that the healthier my body is, the healthier my mind is. I know that a healthy diet, nutritional supplements, and exercise have helped me. I work with a naturopathic physician (a naturopath) and use a variety of holistic approaches. I've found that many of the supplements I take specifically for anxiety do in fact work. And the homeopathic remedies that have been prescribed by my naturopath have had a positive effect on specific problems and overall health. The bottom line is that I keep my mind open to all forms of healing because I want to feel good.

Energy Healing

I was never much into the holistic approach of healing and treatments until I met my wife Jeanine Sande, who is a medical intuitive, a Reiki master, and an energy healer. From my own experience, it seems that more and more people are gravitating toward holistic approaches in conjunction with Western medicine, including acupuncture, acupressure, and Reiki.

Some psychologists practice energy psychology, such as Emotional Freedom Technique (EFT), or tapping, and Eye Movement Desensitization and Reprocessing. I choose to use all the tools available to me to recover from OCD.

Listen, if I really want to get better, I have to keep an open mind.

I married at the age of 50 for the first time. I actually prayed for someone to come into my life who had some form of medical or healing background, some kind of psychological education that hopefully would help her to understand the complex disorder of OCD. I'm not really a big-time praying man. But who showed up in my life? A woman who is a holistic energy healer. *Go figure!*

One of the first things that Jeanine did was introduce me to a naturopath, who holistically looked at the OCD and my entire physiology—including mind, body, and spirit—to better understand me. When the supplements, which were chosen specifically for me, started to have some effect on my anxiety, I became a believer and began to trust this newest "tool" in the healing toolbox.

Next, I started to trust energy healing when I went to a seminar that Jeanine's teacher was presenting. Jeanine's teacher chose me to participate in the demonstration of hands-on healing. In front of the crowd of healers, health professionals, nurses, and others—who, like me, were interested in this art of healing—Jeanine told her teacher about my disorder and the anxiety that had challenged me throughout life. As I lay down on the treatment table, this talented woman gently put her hands on me, focusing on my head.

Now, keep in mind that this had nothing to do with the religious type of healing that you see on television. It was almost clinical and very precise in the way this healer attended to me. After 20 minutes, I was told to slowly get up, drink plenty of water, and take it easy. Jeanine and her friend then walked me around the grounds of the retreat. I know this all sounds weird or bizarre. But I have to tell you that, after the 20-minute treatment from Jeanine's teacher, I honestly felt anxiety-free. I was experiencing a sense of euphoria, complete relaxation, and an overall sense of freedom. This bliss lasted for about four hours and instilled a new belief and trust in energy healing.

I was now open to other holistic approaches to help OCD or, at the very least, my anxiety. I learned a Japanese hands-on healing technique called Reiki, which was something I could use on myself. This, in turn, opened my mind even further and had me thinking, "What other alternative modalities could I look into to calm my nervous system?" I was not racing after any and every potential approach; I was selective. But I kept my mind open, and I tried modalities that I could trust.

Along with Western medicine, I include supplements, meditation, mindful awareness, Reiki, EFT or tapping, good nutrition, and exercise. I'm also open to learning about new and old modalities that make sense to me.

Exercise

I never took exercise quite as seriously as I do now as a treatment for OCD and my overall well-being. It was a pretty simple formula for me: Anxiety produces adrenaline, which made me feel awful and exacerbated OCD symptoms. Exercise burns off adrenaline, calms the nervous system, and creates endorphins, which made me feel better and decreased the symptoms of OCD. And there's scientific proof that backs it up. The hard part for me was sticking to it and not turning exercise into an OCD ritual itself.

My physical therapist turned me on to a book titled *Spark* by John Ratey, MD, also the author of *Driven to Distraction*. *Spark* taught me that exercise and simply increasing your heart rate for a period of time have a positive mind-body connection. Research on neuroplasticity shows that exercise rewires our brains to help shift our mood and can reduce depression and anxiety.

My take on all of this was very clear: I had to get off the couch, get away from the computer, stop feeling sorry for myself, and take a walk! Why should I trust all this? First of all, because it makes me feel good. And feeling good is what I want more of. Also as important, I feel as though I'm taking charge, I'm in control, and I'm doing something to overcome OCD symptoms. So, I'm going to keep exercising and keep on walkin' because they're both part of a treatment and a lifestyle that really works for my mind and body.

Jim's 80-20 Suggestion

I came up with my 80-20 suggestion to remind me that banging the "complaining drum" and being a victim of OCD do me absolutely no good. So, I came up with this approach for myself, which I do perfectly imperfectly.

I'm a big proponent of expression. In fact, when I lecture about OCD, I always tell audiences that the suppression of expression can cause big problems. On the other hand, I have found myself talking incessantly to family members and friends about my problems and trials with OCD. And, quite frankly, they have the capacity to listen to and absorb about 20% of what I'm saying before they tune out or have had enough.

That's not a criticism. I mean, seriously, how much complaining or negativity can one human take? I believe that complaining begets complaining, and negativity begets more negativity. The more I talk and talk and talk about what's wrong, the more power I'm giving to OCD.

Now, when talking with family or friends, I try to catch myself and express my challenges for about 20-30% of the time, which is difficult when OCD can be such an overriding factor in your life. Then the trick becomes what to talk about for the other 70-80% of the time. With time and practice (don't forget, with OCD, we become Grammy winners at banging that "complaining drum"), I forced myself to talk about subjects that felt good to me, that made me laugh, or that felt creative or exciting. Consciously, I pushed myself to listen more and be more responsive to the person with whom I was engaging rather than only talking about myself.

OCD has a big, fat ego. And my new 80-20 suggestion allowed me to deflate some of that power and bad energy and return it back to me. By taking control and only allowing OCD 20% or so, I found a new sense of empowerment. Now I'm in charge. There's a new sheriff in town, and his name is "restraint and prudence." I've also become a much better listener. And that benefits everyone.

That's my 80-20 suggestion.

Nutrition

I remember how, in 1983, after I was released from the hospital and moved into my apartment, I was consumed with exposure challenges. One of my biggest challenges was deciding what to eat.

I had just spent almost six weeks in a psychiatric ward, then a few weeks after that at my parents' house while waiting for my apartment to be ready. I was alone in my apartment. How on earth was I going to shop at a grocery store. And what could I manage to make for myself?

In many ways, it feels like a lifetime ago. But, as I write this, I flash back to that moment. All I could manage was making a grilled cheese sandwich in my toaster oven, being able to take some crackers out of the box, and calling that dinner. Most of the time, though, I would eat out, and Denny's restaurant became a usual hangout. For some magical reason, my mind latched onto the thought that most restaurants were "safe." Then came the frozen food years: three Healthy Choice dinners and a spinach soufflé, two take-out pizzas that I thought were healthy, and some kind of packaged chocolate pudding. Making you hungry?

My God! When I think of what I was putting into my body on a daily basis, it's no wonder that my anxiety was through the roof. I was fueling it with nothing more than sugar and other junk. Remember my experience in the chicken dinner episode (or I should say "How to Wash a Dead Chicken") when I attempted to make a chicken dinner for my girlfriend? That's when I had the breakthrough, when I took the risk of touching food.

I was always grateful for the occasions when my late, great friend Phil Mancini, who owned an Italian deli, would feed me delicious, healthy food while we worked on our movie scripts. Those days I miss.

Research about nutrition and anxiety has increased over the years, including foods to help relieve anxiety and supplements to help manage it.

I chose to work with a naturopath to help me holistically with supplements that helped reduce my anxiety and treat the OCD symptoms. For years, however, it was a trial-and-error process with supplements and homeopathic remedies. But, after all the trial and error, I've come to a good and healthy balance with the help of my naturopath.

Now, no more frozen dinners and crackers for dinner. Not that I have anything against a frozen dinner once in a while. But now that I understand how food and nutrition play such a vital role in overall health, I accept the fact that good nutrition is healing medicine. My diet mostly consists of plenty of salmon, chicken, darker colored vegetables, and whole grains, and doing my best to stay away from refined sugar.

Jeanine also makes one hell of a smoothie filled with lots of good stuff—fruits and veggies, good quality proteins, antioxidants, grains, and seeds. Is it an OCD elixir? No. But it's one of the healthiest things I've had in my diet for years. And, as they say, it can't hurt. Please check with your doctor before making this type of drink. If you are allergic to anything on the list, don't use it. Feel free to add or subtract any ingredients that sound good to you. Bananas and yogurt are good additions that aren't mentioned. Here's the recipe:

Jeanine's "Everything but the Kitchen Sink" Smoothie Recipe

1 tbsp. pumpkin seeds

1 tbsp. flax seeds

1 tbsp. grated coconut

1 tbsp. sunflower seeds

2 tbsp. lecithin granules

1 tbsp. freeze-dried acai berries

1 tbsp. goji berries

half an apple

half a beet with the greens

spinach

parsley

1 carrot

1 stalk celery

1 tbsp. fish oil

2 scoops whey protein powder

1 scoop hemp protein powder

dash of soy milk (unsweetened) or almond milk

water

frozen blueberries and other fruit

a couple of ice cubes

Keep in mind that we have a high-powered blender, which will blend all of this stuff to make a tasty breakfast smoothie.

Finally, I can say that my diet and what I choose to eat have made a huge difference in my ongoing recovery from OCD. It's been an essential part of my journey to feel good and get better. I suggest strongly that you add good nutrition to your recovery tools, and be patient about the outcome. For me, the outcome is paying off. *That* I can trust.

Self-talk and Affirmations

Over the years of being challenged with OCD, I have talked myself down from anxiety and panic more times than I can remember. It's one of the most effective tools in my arsenal. What do I say to myself when I am in the midst of horrible, negative OCD thoughts of disaster? For me, it's a process of challenging or countering each obsession and thought.

Remember the horrible checking compulsion and ritual I had just walking down my street? And how it took me an entire summer to challenge it mindfully? Well, here's another way that I have used to counter the checking obsessions and bring me back to the truth.

I used to see or feel something in the road. And, as I walked past it or over it, I had this incredible, unrelenting urge to "check" or look back and see what it was. Because I have experience in writing plays and screenplays, I wrote a little self-talk dialogue between me and OCD. Please note that those of us who struggle with OCD do *not* hear voices. Let's keep it simple. What happens is that we think thoughts that are irrational, that scare the hell out of us. The kicker is that we know they're irrational, yet we doubt our rational mind. *We just don't trust.*

OCD: "Did you just feel that bump?"

Jim: "Yes, I felt it."

OCD: "Well, you'd better look back and check to see if it was something that got on your shoe."

Jim: "Nah, it was just a bump in the road."

OCD: "It could've been a bump in the road, or it could've been some dog shit. And you stepped in it."

Jim: "Nice try, OCD. I thought you thought it was a bump?"

OCD: "Then it could have been a small animal that you stepped on and killed. And you're responsible for that."

Jim: "You're really stretching here. Do you have any idea how many bumps there are in this road? Besides, if I stepped on an animal, I guarantee you that I would've heard something. You see, OCD, I don't have a lot of control over what gets under my feet."

OCD (with an insistent tone): "You just caused the death of an innocent bug. And you have to live with the guilt for the rest of your life. You know you won't be able to walk this street or any street without checking every step you take."

Jim: "Cut the drama. You bring up this death talk every time. Is that your default setting to scare me? Thanks for sharing. But I'm not buying your crap. I've seen many people on this road, and none of them are checking under their feet. None of them care. None of them think the way you do. Even if I hadn't seen others walk this path, the bottom line is that you are OCD. Your job is to make me doubt. Seriously, would *you* trust you? I choose to trust that this world doesn't operate the way you are telling me it operates."

OCD: "Well, it's blood on your hands or on your shoes. Either way, you are guilty again."

Jim: "You are not my friend. And I don't trust anything you say. I trust my own thoughts, my own reality. And, no matter what thought you've put into my head, I'm going to keep walking."

I *did* keep walking and affirmed to myself, "I am walking. I am choosing to trust myself, not OCD. I will keep going, no matter what." And, as you have read, after a summer of ERP and self-talk, I now rarely get stuck checking.

Sometimes the words in the dialog are different, or in a different order. But the idea here is to *trust your own truth.* And OCD doesn't have much of a chance when you counter it with a consistent barrage of truth.

Affirmations have made a big difference in my recovery. Whether I believe them or not, my subconscious mind will gradually come to believe the words I am saying. And that helps me heal and remember where I want to be. Here are a few of my favorite affirmations:

- "I choose peace."
- "Every time I challenge OCD, I weaken it."
- "I trust that I am bigger than OCD."
- "I trust I am more powerful than OCD."
- "I trust that I am healthier than I think."
- "I choose to stay in the moment."
- "I choose to change because nothing changes if nothing changes."
- "I trust that my body will take care of me."
- "I trust that there are far more good people than bad."

- "I trust that I will heal."
- "I choose to trust reality."
- "I choose love over fear."
- "Let go and let God."
- "Regardless of what I see, think, or feel, I keep going."
- "I choose to listen to my inner voice of reason."
- "Slow down and trust."
- "I'm going to do just what's in front of me."
- "One step at a time."
- "The only way over fear is through it."
- "I choose to stop complaining and start reframing into the positive."
- "I choose to fake it until I make it."
- "I am love."
- "I am peace."
- "I will be free."
- "I TRUST."

In my life, I have used affirmations and self-talk as healing tools. I've written many of these affirmations and slogans on sheets of paper and Post-its and put them on my walls. Then, in a moment's notice, I can be reminded of what my truth is.

It helps to remember that I have the power to know I'm in charge. I'm not just sitting back and letting OCD bully me. I'm actively doing something to help myself. Even if I don't believe the affirmations, I still say them because, in time, they do sink in. And I begin to trust them. It's really about using them as a conscious tool to shift your thoughts. *That* I can trust. It feels right. And it feels good.

Reasonable Reason to Change

A "reasonable reason to change" is an interesting and powerful concept for me. It made the most sense when I first heard it in a lecture by Dr. Wayne Dyer from his book, *Excuses Begone!: How to Change Lifelong, Self-Defeating Thinking Habits*, which I highly recommend. Throughout my life, when I struggled to accept rational reasoning, OCD always matched it with doubt. I would try to rationalize a reason to change my behaviors. But OCD would argue with a "yes, but" and a "what if."

I was stuck in what Dr. Jeffrey Schwartz calls "brain lock." In his book, *Brain Lock: Free Yourself from Obsessive-Compulsive Behavior,* Dr. Schwartz describes OCD as a result of a biochemical imbalance in the brain, where thoughts will get "locked" in an obsessive-compulsive loop. I have been in that loop many, many times. So, when I am in those awful loops, how can I possibly bring myself to change anything, let alone think about a "reasonable reason to change"? It is just too overwhelming at those times.

As I have studied my challenges with the disorder, it has become very clear to me that when I have a *reason*—not just a thought but a *reasonable reason* to work harder at ERP—I go for it with more motivation, and then shift to face the fear.

My challenges have always been related to germs, which have manifested in taking obsessively long showers, rituals around going to the bathroom for far too long, washing my hands too much, checking rituals, obsessions about harming. And ... well, you know the rest if you've gotten this far in the book.

I'll give you an example of one of my "reasonable reasons" that has helped me to move a little faster in the bathroom. First of all, if I wanted to continue to live in a nice house by the ocean and have the income that I'm accustomed to, which includes medical benefits that I truly need for two therapists and a family doctor, I needed to work and do my best to get there on time. Is that a "reasonable reason" to feel the fear and do it anyway, as Susan Jeffers' book, *Feel the Fear ... and Do It Anyway*, so aptly states? *You're damn right, it is!*

I've talked about my wife Jeanine in this book. She is a beautiful soul with a compassionate spirit, who also likes to have fun as do I. Is having wonderful fun times with Jeanine a "reasonable reason" to take more risks around my fears and work harder at my recovery? *Absolutely!*

When I take more risks around my fears, and trust that it is all for my higher good, it's always successful in some way or another. Even if for one hour, it's a tiny bit better. So, how does this work? I believe that my brain processes the *reason*, decides that it is *reasonable*, and then moves me into action.

I found an interesting aspect to all of this: If I simply set the intention, and imagine myself changing and moving toward my fear, that starts the positive momentum. For instance, I imagine writing more books, making the movie that's been in my head for over 30 years, and doing more service to help others with OCD because it makes me feel good. I put these intentions into my imagination and hold them there. And I don't let them go, no matter what. I then find myself risking a little more, walking my talk a little bit more. And, most of all, remembering to listen to my inner voice that says, "I want to get better."

Some days this absolutely works; other, more stressful days, I have trouble finding that reason, that motivation or positive inner voice. And OCD wants to fight. Let me put it this way: OCD despises it when I think in recovery terms. It hates it when I challenge its meaningless obsessions and compulsions by taking the risk to stop and feel all the feelings of anxiety until they dissipate. OCD is one, big, damn bully that wants its way, or it's going to threaten more anxiety. But, let's face it, bullies are bullies. They kick and scream for what they want. When that OCD bully threatens me with an anxious thought, I'm not going to give it what it wants. I need to remember all my tools and my reasons to change, and stand as strong as I can with my intentions. When I do, the bully *always* cowers.

Nothing Changes if Nothing Changes

My recovery is based on change. In my heart and mind, I know that the only way I will gain real recovery is to change. OCD hates change. But my inner voice or intuition knows that I need to shift and change the self-defeating behaviors. My best example is the shower ritual. Let me give you a bit more detail about the ERP process for the shower.

As you know, I've worked with my wife and ERP coach Jeanine for years to cut down the time in the shower from literally an hour and 15 minutes to a total of 13 minutes.

Why? Because I got sick and tired of being sick and tired. And it was reasonable for me to take a shower in the approximate time the general public does. I looked it up. John Q. Public's average shower takes 8-10 minutes, using approximately 50 gallons of water.

I allowed myself to trust Jeanine completely. I mean, there was no doubting her. This is how we did it. Jeanine rehearsed with me, taking a 10-minute "shower" away from the bathroom—actually, it was in our living room, fully clothed and basically pantomiming the process. I videotaped it all. I was determined to go for it and wanted a visual record of how to change. Then I had Jeanine videotape me taking the new and improved 10-minute shower. I wanted a record of this too, so I could look back and retrain my brain how to change.

Guess what? I took the shower in 10 minutes and had very little anxiety after the shower. What I did experience, however, was a surge of excitement, accomplishment, and finally some hope! From an hour and 15 minutes to 10 minutes! C'mon. You've *got* to be impressed. How did I make that change? It's called "unconditional trust."

After a few days of my mastering the 10-minute shower, Jeanine playfully named it "the Top-Down Jim Shower!"

I found myself saying, "This is reasonable" and "I can do it."

Unconditional trust in my coach, with a reasonable reason to change, suddenly made sense to me. You can do this too, with any obsession or compulsion. The trick is to trust unconditionally. For me, it meant that I had to put full, unconditional trust into what Jeanine was suggesting, and then practice that trust by reviewing my video. My brain adapted after some time, and I could then take the shorter shower on my own. I have found that there is no in between when it comes to trusting. I trust, or I don't trust. That's it. *No conditions.*

Hope

I can't say enough about the word "hope." You've seen that word throughout this book because I know the word "hope" has positive energy. Hope is a powerful feeling that motivates me into action. It is my strong belief that, no matter how bad or serious OCD is, there is always hope—always! When there is hope—whether it is coming from your higher power; your inner self; or a "champion" like your ERP coach, therapist, friend, family member, or even someone in an online OCD support group—it is the most powerful and indestructible defense against OCD.

When I feel hope, I feel healing.

When I feel hope, I feel love.

When I feel hope, I feel my life coming home again.

It doesn't take much. A little hope goes a long way.

I also believe that, when you receive hope, you must pass it on. Give hope to someone in return. Call someone who is suffering with OCD, join an OCD chat room, write a blog about your recovery, or offer some type of positive reinforcement. Believe me, you will get hope back in return.

I think of hope as a verb! You've got to find it and give it. I do my best each day to get some form of hope and inspiration by listening to CDs about hope, watching any film or television show that gives me feelings of hope, talking with others about problems and not about solutions. It all translates into healing. I promise you.

Does all of this sound too idealistic? It did for me when I first started my quest for hope. It sounded like one, big, obnoxious Hallmark commercial. However, once I quieted my resistance and actually found that some of those Hallmark commercials about hope were actually working in my life, I became open to accepting hope, or the feeling of hope, from wherever I could get it.

Therefore, I encourage you to try these actions:

- Refuse to believe that there is no hope.
- If you are feeling hopeless, stop, relax, breathe, and begin imagining hope.
- Imagine hope in your life, and then feel the feelings around it. Hold onto those feelings for they are real.
- Search out hope wherever you can, take it, and then give it away.
- Always give hope to others for it will come back tenfold.
- Never *ever* give up hope.
- Always trust that, no matter what happens in life, there is always hope.

The Opposite of Fear Is Trust

In this chapter, I wanted to include what Phil said to me so many years ago, which I've been thinking about lately. The opposite of fear could be thought of as bravery or courage.

But, in the context of OCD, he said, "The opposite of fear is trust."

If we truly trust—and I mean that intuitive trust in anything—we will not fear. After all these years of writing and lecturing on the premise that "the opposite of fear is trust," I have added that the opposite of fear is also love. Let me put it this way: In my life experience, when I feel a "loving trust," there is no reason to fear. I encourage you to *be* that "loving trust" in all walks of your life. And you may no longer need to seek it out as it *will* come to you. You can transcend your fears.

Trust that: You can have a meaningful life while living with OCD. In the beginning, I didn't think so. But, when I started working with even one of these tools, I got a little better, and then a little more better. And then I even found I could have a good life—living with OCD.

The most important thing I have learned is that OCD is *part* of my life; it's not *all* of my life.

CHAPTER 17

How I Am Now, Living with OCD

You teach best what you most need to learn.

~ Richard Bach

After all the tools I have learned, after all the therapy and spirituality I have embraced, I can tell you that I have come to a much different place in my recovery. I don't fight OCD like I did so passionately in the beginning. Fighting with a biological disorder and myself may have served me then. But I now choose acceptance, patience, and compassion for myself rather than the black-and-white thinking that OCD tries so hard to make me believe. You see, it's not black and white. It's not, "If I'm not cured from OCD, I won't have a life." It sure felt like that in 1982 though. I had no idea how to live with this.

The good news is that there is a middle ground. By focusing on recovery and using the many tools that helped me move forward, I found a grey area where I could *manage and accept OCD as part of my life*. It's the same as someone managing and living with depression, diabetes, arthritis, or any other chronic disease or disorder. I'm living with OCD and getting better every day I challenge it, knowing that, when I challenge it, I weaken it. I can and do have a happy and productive life. And I now see OCD as only a shadow and not the truth. And certainly nothing I can trust.

Do I still have tough days? Of course, I do! And that's the time when I have the opportunity to use any and all of my tools in this book.

Is OCD still a big part of me? I can confidently say that it is *not*.

I choose to not be defined by OCD. Anxiety waves in and out of my life, depending on stress. But I have a life. I am living with OCD and taking one step at a time toward feeling better in any given moment. And I do cherish those moments with a deeper gratitude and appreciation than ever before. Sometimes it's two steps forward and one back. But only *one* back.

I now look at OCD recovery as a very part-time job. There are days when I feel ungrounded, foggy, kind of like an "out of body—who am I?" feeling. I do my best to ignore it because I know it's just the overwhelm of anxiety. And it will pass. When it does, I find myself coming back to hope. *Always come back to hope.*

Yes, I do my daily ERP, which only strengths me. But it's not a full-time job anymore. I still have phobias and compulsions that challenge me daily. But I have the tools in my back pocket, so to speak, at all times. The bottom line is this: *I'm living with OCD and having a full life.*

Can you have a job, a relationship, a house, happiness, and still be living with OCD? I have come to trust that the answer to this question is absolutely "yes" with one condition: that you are steadfast in taking even the tiniest steps to move forward.

Research to find better treatments and hopefully a full cure to the disorder is encouraging to me. Gene research, medication alternatives, and new treatments are all promising. I have hope. But, in the meantime, I do my best to walk my talk—taking one step at a time.

Trust and always remember: The brain changes for the better when you face your fears.

CHAPTER 18

How Do We Trust?

Remember, there are no mistakes, only lessons. Love yourself, trust your choices, and everything is possible.

~ Cherie-Carter Scott

From 30+ years of living with OCD, I have come to learn and trust some absolute truths about this disorder and about my life. Although the journey has been challenging, and at times very tough, and while I wouldn't wish this illness on anyone, I can now say that, in many ways, OCD has been a gift.

I know you probably cringed when you read that. How on Earth can such a debilitating, disruptive illness be a *gift*? Let me rephrase: OCD itself is not a gift. But the moments of light, of awareness, that have come from dealing with this illness have brought a strength and wisdom that I might not have otherwise known. Out of this struggle came a resilience that I now have. What came as a result of OCD was empathy, compassion, and knowing myself much more deeply than ever before.

I invite OCD to leave me all the time but not with the same desperation as before. I now accept that it came into my life and taught me many lessons about myself. More importantly, I now know and trust who is in charge: It's me, not OCD.

Am I saying that if I had a choice between a life with OCD or without, I would have chosen with? Are you kidding? *No!* I certainly could have done with a lot less pain, thank you very much. However, I didn't have a choice. So, with this disorder came those unexpected gifts that have changed my life in positive ways.

I've come to absolutely trust some important facts about this often overwhelming disorder. What I can absolutely trust is that OCD puts meaning into meaningless things. It tries to convince me to be fearful and anxious over the "what ifs" of life rather than the truths of life. It wants and demands certainty in an uncertain world. I have said this before, but it's worth repeating: Not one OCD fear that I have had since 1982 has ever come true. Not one. *Ever.*

I *absolutely trust* that OCD lies or distorts the truth. And it's my job to be aware of those lies and trust my inner voice of reason. If I'm in a state where I'm not capable of trusting my own voice of reason, I trust others such as my therapist or coach. I sort of borrow their brain. It's that simple. I call it a "retraining of the brain" or, more accurately, a remembering of what I always knew. For me, healing really began when I stopped trusting OCD and started trusting the truth.

I *absolutely trust* that the only way to push my way through OCD and into recovery is through the "gold standard" for OCD treatment: CBT and ERP. Both of these approaches have been vital to my recovery. They have helped my brain turn a "what if" into a "so what?" Medication and alternative approaches have also helped me.

I *absolutely trust* that I had to get "sick and tired of being sick and tired" to be willing to change. "Nothing changes if nothing changes" is a slogan I trust.

I *absolutely trust* there is a part of me that is bigger than OCD and can transcend it. I've seen it happen. And I work for it daily.

I *absolutely trust* and know that it takes courage and strength to challenge OCD, even in the smallest of ways, and that it can be done.

I *absolutely trust* that the only time we have is the present. The past is gone, the future is only imagined, and being present is crucial to my recovery. I must catch myself whenever I start to obsess about a projected OCD frightening future. *Now* is the only time I have. *Now* is the only time we all have.

Remember what I wrote earlier about "Aunt Bee" and her comment that so resonated with me and changed how I looked at OCD and my recovery? She said, "You can start your day at any time." These words still hold true for me today. They can for you too. It means that you can start or restart your recovery any day, anytime. There is no statute of limitations on the healing process. I also know with all certainty that the core treatment to what once was called "the doubting disease" is trust. *turn doubt to trust*

When I first met Phil and Ron, how and why did I trust them almost immediately? When I first met my wife Jeanine, why did I feel a sense of trust? Well, by now you know that I'm no guru and not qualified to answer the universal question, "How do we trust?" For me, it's as simple as a gut feeling, an intuition that reassures your mind and heart. When I feel it, I do my best to trust and believe it. It hasn't failed me yet.

I chose to trust Phil, Ron, my wife, and all the people who have helped me on this journey because I felt a deep connection with them from the get-go and recognized each as the extraordinary human beings they were. I wanted to be more like them. They inspired me. They gave me hope. I connected with their humor, compassion, kindness, stillness, and ability to listen—but especially their unconditional love.

The word "namaste" (pronounced nam-a-stay) comes from the Sanskrit word *namah-te*. It is usually a greeting of hello or goodbye. But it can have many meanings. One of the meanings that I particularly like is "You and I are One." That's the feeling I get when I trust. It's a oneness. It can be with a person, place, or thing. You name it. Nature, especially where there is water, is a wonderful connection to oneness for me. If I allow myself to respect the present, be in the moment, and let go of that pesky, screaming bully of OCD, I find that I can trust unconditionally. There is no pathway to trust; trust is the path.

In writing this book and simultaneously continuing my recovery process, I came to a hard truth: When it comes to OCD recovery, you either trust or you don't. It's that simple. I had to trust what my therapists were suggesting I do to get better. I had to trust my wife's new instructions for taking a shower. I had to trust that life did not work the way OCD told me it worked. Mostly, I had to trust that I was stronger than I thought.

I want to repeat a line that I wrote at the beginning of this final chapter: I *absolutely trust* and know that it takes courage and strength to challenge OCD, even in the smallest of ways, and that it can be done. Always remember: The opposites of fear are trust and love.

I leave you for now with the hope that this book will, in some way, help you with your challenges and recovery from OCD, and that it can be one of your healing "tools"—a companion of hope as you continue your journey. We can do this together. We are both going to be okay. Try to trust that.

Years ago, my mentor gave me a mantra—"I choose peace"—that you can use anytime when you feel anxious or in pain.

Now, I would like to give you this mantra, which you can trust: "In this moment, I can do it. I will do it. I am capable."

... because you are.

You and I are one.

Namaste, Jim

My Anxiety
First-Aid List

- Take medication, supplements, or other alternative holistic approaches if appropriate, always under your doctors' care.
- Turn on a light. Bring light to darkness.
- Breathe in (letting your stomach expand) while thinking "I choose," and then exhale slowly while thinking "peace." Repeat these words until you calm down a bit.
- Call someone or visit an online support group. A voice or message can soothe you in a moment and remind you what to do. You are not alone!
- Refocus with music, positive movies, TV, or the Internet, including Facebook. The point is to shift your focus away from anxiety and into the present.
- Move a little or a lot, or eat and drink a little something, to shift the anxiety. I usually eat a little fruit (e.g., a banana) or some toast with almond butter. Eat or drink what helps you. I stay away from the obvious anxiety makers (e.g., caffeine, alcohol, and sugar).
- Do just what is in front of you; that is, make no big decisions right now (e.g., "I'm watching TV, so that's

what I'm doing, and I don't need to do anything more"). Think small.

- Make a gratitude list in your mind or on paper (e.g., "I am grateful that I can breathe," "I am grateful that I have a place to live," "I am grateful that I can walk," or "I am grateful that I have a support group"). List as many grateful things that you can think of, and start small. This refocuses the mind and energy for the better.
- Trust that the anxiety will pass. It's just energy, and all energy passes if you allow it.
- Look at something beautiful every day. This could be as simple as looking at a photograph, a painting, or any natural beauty outside. Look at whatever makes you feel better.
- For me, getting outside into nature always soothes me. To find your nature, get into nature.
- Use EFT or tapping. EFT has really helped me. Search EFT on YouTube to learn more.
- Know that, if you decide to do none of the above, anxiety will still calm down with time.
- Hold on to trust right now. Keep the faith a little. It's going to pass. *Really.*

Help and Hope Resources

Foundations and Associations

International OCD Foundation (iocdf.org)
Awareness Foundation for OCD (afocd.org)
Anxiety and Depression Association of America (adaa.org)
National Alliance on Mental Illness (nami.org)
Peace of Mind Foundation (peaceofmind.com)
The A2A Alliance: adversity 2 advocacy (a2aalliance.org)

Treatment Centers and Online Help

The Anxiety Treatment Center
(anxietytreatmentexperts.com)
Anxiety Treatment Services (anxietytreatmentservices.com)
McLean Hospital, Harvard Medical School Affiliate, OCD
Institute (mcleanhospital.org/programs/obsessive-compulsive-disorder-institute-ocdi)
OCD Center of Los Angeles (ocdla.com)
OCD Treatment Centre (ocdtreatmentcentre.com)
Rogers Memorial Hospital, Obsessive-Compulsive
Disorder Center (rogershospital.org/residential-center/obsessive-compulsive-disorder-center)
Stanford School of Medicine: Obsessive-Compulsive and
Related Disorders (ocd.stanford.edu)

12-Step Programs

Co-Dependents Anonymous International (coda.org)
Obsessive Compulsive Anonymous
    (obsessivecompulsiveanonymous.org)

James Callner Films and Coaching Videos

- *The Touching Tree* (a film about a boy with OCD)
- *The Risk* (a film about a family member with OCD)
- *In the Shoes of Christopher* (a film about bullying a teen with OCD)
- OCD Coaching Videos (short videos specifically designed to help those with OCD)

Films and OCD Coaching Videos can be found on YouTube (search for James Callner OCD Channel to view and subscribe), Facebook (facebook.com/ocdcoaching), OCD Treatment Centre (ocdtreatmentcentre.com), and The Awareness Foundation for OCD (afocd.org).

Recommended Books

Adams, Gail, EdD. *Students with OCD: A Handbook for School Personnel.* New York: Pherson Creek Press, 2011.

Baer, Lee, PhD. *Getting Control: Overcoming Your Obsessions and Compulsions.* New York: Plume, 2012.

Beattie, Melody. *The Language of Letting Go: Daily Meditations for Codependents.* Center City, MN: Hazelden, 1990.

Buscaglia, Leo F. *Love: What Life Is All About.* New York: Ballantine Books, 1996.

Dyer, Wayne W. *Excuses Begone!: How to Change Lifelong, Self-Defeating Thinking Habits,* 4th ed. Carlsbad, CA: Hay House, 2011.

____. *Living the Wisdom of the Tao: The Complete Tao Te Ching and Affirmations.* Carlsbad, CA: Hay House, 2008.

Grayson, Jonathan, PhD. *Freedom from Obsessive Compulsive Disorder.* New York: Berkley, 2014.

Hershfield, Jon, MFT, and Jeff Bell. *When a Family Member Has OCD: Mindfulness & Cognitive Behavioral Skills to Help Families Affected by Obsessive Compulsive Disorder.* Oakland, CA: New Harbinger Publications, 2015.

Hershfield, Jon, MFT, and Tom Corboy, MFT. *The Mindfulness Workbook for OCD: A Guide to Overcoming*

Obsessions and Compulsions Using Mindfulness and Cognitive Behavioral Therapy. Oakland, CA: New Harbinger Publications, 2013.

Hyman, Bruce M., PhD, LCSW, and Cherlene Pedrick, RN. *The OCD Workbook: Your Guide to Breaking Free from Obsessive-Compulsive Disorder,* 3rd ed. Oakland, CA: New Harbinger Publications, 2010.

Jeffers, Susan, PhD. *Feel the Fear … and Do It Anyway,* 20th anniversary ed. New York: Ballantine Books, 2006.

Schwartz, Jeffrey M., and Beverly Beyette. *Brain Lock: Free Yourself from Obsessive-Compulsive Behavior.* New York: Harper Perennial, 1997.

Tolle, Eckhart. *The Power of Now: A Guide to Spiritual Enlightenment.* Vancouver: Namaste Publishing, 2004.

ABOUT THE AUTHOR

James Callner, MA

 James Callner's onset of OCD came in his 20s. To this day, he continues his recovery with CBT/ERP, spiritual, medical, and holistic therapies and treatments, and has emerged as an educator and a public speaker specializing in OCD and anxiety.

Mr. Callner started his college teaching and professional filmmaking career in his early 20s. He has earned over 30 national and international film festival awards as well as critical acclaim for writing and directing films about physically and emotionally challenged individuals. He was commissioned by the International OCD Foundation to make the first dramatic educational film about a child with OCD, *The Touching Tree*.

He went on to make *In the Shoes of Christopher*, a dramatic film about OCD and bullying; *The Risk*, a film about OCD and the family; and *Hope and Solutions for OCD*, a four-part lecture series with OCD professionals. All films can be found on afocd.org and YouTube.

Mr. Callner currently provides inspiration and recovery techniques through his OCD Coaching Videos and Words of Hope, and his articles can be found on afocd.org, Facebook, YouTube, and other social media. He is cofounder and president of the Awareness Foundation for OCD as well as OCD Education and Media Specialist for the OCD Treatment Centre (ocdtreatmentcentre.com). James Callner lives with his wife Jeanine by the ocean in northern California.

ABOUT THE EDITOR

Jan Baumgartner

 A native Californian, Jan Baumgartner is a writer, an essayist, and a creative content book editor. Primarily a travel writer, she's also worked as a grant writer for the nonprofit sector in the fields of academia, AIDS, and wildlife conservation for NGOs in the United States and Africa.

Her numerous articles and essays have been published online and in print, both nationally and abroad, and include travel writing for *The New York Times*. Her diverse writing topics range from ALS, human rights, Africa, wildlife/endangered species conservation, humor/satire, and solo travel around the globe. Her essays on Mexico are published in two anthologies.

Following her passion, she has traveled extensively in Africa, Europe, Mexico, and beyond; most recently, she participated in a three-month, home-exchange adventure between Paris, Tuscany, and Istanbul, Turkey. She lives in San Miguel de Allende, Mexico.

Made in the USA
Middletown, DE
13 July 2018